U.S. CYBER DIPLOMACY IN AN ERA OF GROWING THREATS

HEARING

BEFORE THE

COMMITTEE ON FOREIGN AFFAIRS
HOUSE OF REPRESENTATIVES

ONE HUNDRED FIFTEENTH CONGRESS

SECOND SESSION

FEBRUARY 6, 2018

Serial No. 115–106

Printed for the use of the Committee on Foreign Affairs

Available via the World Wide Web: http://www.foreignaffairs.house.gov/ or
http://www.gpo.gov/fdsys/

U.S. GOVERNMENT PUBLISHING OFFICE

28–539PDF   WASHINGTON : 2018

CONTENTS

Page

WITNESSES

LETTERS, STATEMENTS, ETC., SUBMITTED FOR THE HEARING

APPENDIX

U.S. CYBER DIPLOMACY IN AN ERA OF GROWING THREATS

TUESDAY, FEBRUARY 6, 2018

House of Representatives,
Committee on Foreign Affairs,
Washington, DC.

The committee met, pursuant to notice, at 10:09 a.m. in room 2172, Rayburn, House Office Building, Hon. Ed Royce (chairman of the committee) presiding.

Chairman Royce. We will call the hearing to order and ask all the members to take their seats. This is on U.S. cyber diplomacy. Cyberattacks and commercial espionage and ransomware used by foreign governments, used by terrorists, used by criminals, are a serious threat to our U.S. national security. They are also a threat to our economic interests around the globe, of course.

As the intelligence community made clear in the 2017 Worldwide Threat Assessment:

> "Our adversaries are becoming more adept at using cyberspace to threaten our interests and advance their own. And despite improving our cyber defenses, nearly all information, communication networks, and systems will be at risk for years."

Cyber threats have, of course, real-world impact. And in 2015, Chinese hackers stole the personnel files of 20 million current and former Federal employees in a massive data breach. And last year, North Korean hackers crippled hospitals in the United Kingdom, and they also halted international shipping in India. Russia exploits cyberspace to attack its neighbors, including Estonia and Ukraine, and to attempt to undermine Western democracies, including the United States. Yes, our military does have some very unique offensive and defensive capabilities in cyberspace, and other agencies to protect our critical infrastructure have as well. But it is our diplomats who work with our allies and partners to develop a common response to these threats, and they do that while engaging our adversaries to make clear that cyberattacks resulting in real-world consequences will be viewed by us as a use of force.

The importance of the State Department's work cannot be understated. Indeed, the Department's role becomes essential when you consider that it is not just computer networks and infrastructure that the United States needs to protect. The open nature of the Internet is increasingly under assault by authoritarian regimes, regimes like China, that aggressively promote a vision of cyber sov-

(1)

ereignty. And this vision emphasizes State control over cyberspace. This, obviously, could lead to a totalitarian dystopia. It obviously runs counter to American values of individual and economic liberty. And we know what that could mean, for example, to the people of China or other countries.

We saw this recently in Iran. We saw the regime shut down mobile Internet access, and saw them block and pressure companies to cut off social media tools that were used by the people of Iran to organize themselves and to publicize protests among the people of Iran. Authoritarian regimes would love to globalize this censorship. And that is the goal here, to globalize censorship. That is the kind of censorship they have long-imposed at home, and they would like to entice and empower authoritarian regimes around the world to do the same thing.

So it falls to our diplomats to help ensure the world rejects this limited version of cyberspace and that the American vision of an open, secure, innovative Internet wins out over George Orwell's premonitions.

Coordination among allies is critical in response to different undertakings of privacy between—and understandings between the United States and Europe. The State Department will work with the Department of Commerce to successfully negotiate the EU-U.S. privacy shield framework. And this ensures the data and business continues to flow across the Atlantic. And just yesterday, this House passed a bill strengthening our cyber coordination with Ukraine. But there is much more to be done.

And that is why last month, the House passed the Cyber Diplomacy Act. This bill, which I introduced, ensures that the State Department has a senior diplomat charged with leading this effort that brings together our security, human rights, and economic priorities. And I am encouraged to hear that the administration has heard our concerns and is working to elevate this position.

So today, we are joined by three experts with experience in cyber diplomacy, technology, and defense, including the Department's former Coordinator for Cyber Issues.

We look forward to discussing how Congress can best support strong cyber diplomacy. And with that, I turn to our ranking member, Mr. Engel, for his opening statement.

Mr. ENGEL. Thank you, Mr. Chairman, for convening this hearing. And to our witnesses, welcome to the Foreign Affairs Committee. I look forward to hearing your thoughts on how the United States should improve its cybersecurity policy and address the cyber threats we face from overseas.

America's adversaries are becoming bolder and more sophisticated as they pursue their aims in cyberspace. This is a challenge for our technology community, a new frontier for our diplomats, and a threat to our security. It is also an economic hazard with American businesses standing to lose out in the face of hostile and unscrupulous behavior in cyberspace. Iran's attacks on America's infrastructure, including a dam near my district in New York, and North Korea's attack on the entertainment sector underscored troubling vulnerabilities to this sort of tactic.

We reached a 2015 agreement with China to prevent cyber theft of intellectual property. But Beijing still exerts more and more state control over the Internet, denying its citizens basic freedoms and hurting American business. The United States is not working closely enough with like-minded governments to deter adversaries from stealing secrets or undermining an open and interoperable Internet. And, of course, Russia's cyberattacks were the centerpiece of its attack on American democracy during the 2016 Presidential election.

On this last point, frankly, I am stunned by the administration's utter failure to respond to these attacks. More than a year has gone by since the intelligence community revealed the extent of Russian meddling. Congress overwhelmingly passed new sanctions, new legislation to give the White House tools to punish those responsible. The law singles out those responsible for cyber crimes. It goes after the military and intelligence sectors that drove this attack. Yet the Trump administration has not imposed a single sanction related to election interference mandated by the law. The decision to completely ignore Congress' intent and blow up last week's deadline for new sanctions has made that much worse by what administration officials themselves admit, and that is, Russia is at it again.

The CIA Director, a former Member of Congress, a former colleague, Mike Pompeo, has said so repeatedly, which calls into question the State Department's claim that just a threat of sanctions alone will deter bad behavior. I am at a loss. We are talking about the bedrock of American democracy, and the administration seems intent on signaling to Russia and the rest of the world that it is open season. Between the President's constant denial of Russia's involvement and his constant attacks on our own justice system, you would almost conclude that he would be fine with a repeat of what we saw in 2016. Well, I am not fine with it. The President won't take steps to protect American democracy. It falls to us as lawmakers.

Last year I introduced a bill with Mr. Connolly, the SECURE Our Democracy Act, which would specifically go after those who interfere with an American election from overseas. When we passed the sanctions package last summer, we put this bill aside because we thought the President would use the tools we gave him to push back against Russian aggression. He didn't, so now I think it is time to reconsider this measure or something similar.

Responding to Russia is just one piece of the puzzle when it comes to our cyber policy. I also think we need to reverse course on the administration's relentless assault on our diplomacy and development. Mr. Painter, I am sorry that you were one casualty of the administration's attempt to hollow out the State Department when you were forced out of your role as Coordinator for Cyber Issues. This was a major blow to American leadership at a time when your expertise was needed the most. I was speaking with Mr. Keating just before, and we were lamenting about the fact about how the administration has really not sent us the witnesses that we really feel that we could use so they could give us the perspective from the executive branch.

So I was glad to join Chairman Royce to introduce the Cyber Diplomacy Act, which would reinstate and elevate the position, your position, Mr. Painter. It passed the House a few weeks ago, and I

4

hope the Senate acts on it soon. And I hope it sends a message to the administration that we need to ramp up our diplomacy on cyber, not scale it back. We need to engage with friendly governments facing the same threats. We need to push back against countries that will exploit these tools to pilfer our intellectual property to hack into our country's most sensitive information and to derail international norms to keep the Internet open and accessible.

So I hope that our witnesses can shed additional light on these concerns and share with this committee their views on how the United States can lead on this issue.

So I thank you again, Mr. Chairman, and I yield back.

Chairman ROYCE. Thank you, Mr. Engel.

So this morning we are pleased to be joined by a distinguished panel, including Mr. Chris Painter. As you mentioned, he serves as the Global Commissioner for the Stability of Cyberspace, and previously was the first Coordinator for Cyber Issues at the State Department. We also have John Miller, Vice President for Global Policy and Law, Cybersecurity, and Privacy at the Information Technology Industry Council. And we have Dr. Michael Sulmeyer, Belfer Center's Cybersecurity Project Director at the Harvard Kennedy School. Previously, he served as the Director for Plans and Operations for Cyber Policy in the Office of the Secretary of Defense.

So without objection, the witnesses' full prepared statements are going to be made part of the record, and all the members here, you are going to have 5 calendar days to submit any other statements or questions or extraneous material that you want in the record.

We have been informed that votes may come earlier this morning than we anticipated, so we want as many members as possible to have a chance to ask their questions. And to that end, members and witnesses, please respect the 5-minute time limit.

So if you would, Mr. Painter, if you could summarize your remarks, we will begin with you.

STATEMENT OF MR. CHRISTOPHER PAINTER, COMMISSIONER, GLOBAL COMMISSION FOR THE STABILITY OF CYBERSPACE (FORMER COORDINATOR FOR CYBER ISSUES, U.S. DEPARTMENT OF STATE)

Mr. PAINTER. Chairman Royce, Ranking Member Engel, members of the House Foreign Affairs Committee, it is a pleasure to be here today to discuss the growing technical and policy threats in cyberspace and the vital role of diplomacy in combating those threats and shaping an international environment that promotes an open, interoperable, secure, and reliable information infrastructure.

For over 26 years, I have devoted my life to these issues serving in senior roles in the Department of Justice, the National Security Council, and, most recently, as the first Coordinator for Cyber Issues at the State Department. I continue to work on these issues after leaving government, including serving as a Commissioner on the Global Commission for the Stability of Cyberspace, and a board member for the Center for Internet Security.

Over the course of my career, I have seen the technical threats in cyberspace posed by state and non-state actors dramatically increase in both sophistication and number, and have seen the potential and actual impact of those threats grow exponentially. I have also seen the rise of serious policy threats to the very nature, structure, and governance of the Internet as we know it. Unprecedented attempts to undermine democratic processes, threats posed to economic prosperity, and the increasing drive by repressive regimes to suppress and control online discourse and undermine Internet freedom.

It is clear that responding to cyber threats and seizing the many opportunities in cyberspace requires a whole-of-government response leveraging the capabilities of agencies across the Federal Government in working with the private sector and civil society. It is also clear, given the international nature of the threats and the technology itself, that the State Department must play a leading role in that effort, and that effective cyber diplomacy is paramount.

The United States has provided significant leadership in this area in the past. Indeed, my former office, the Office of the Coordinator for Cyber Issues, the first of its kind anywhere in the world, literally created and advanced a whole new area of foreign policy focus that simply did not exist before, and made substantial progress in the number of policy and operational fronts.

Over 25 countries have followed our example by establishing high level positions in their foreign ministries. For the U.S. to continue to lead as it must, cyber issues must be re-prioritized and appropriately resourced at the State Department. Among other things, effective cyber diplomacy involves, one, building strategic partnerships with other countries around the world and engaging the many, many multilateral forms that are shaping cyber policy; two, using diplomacy and diplomatic tools to directly respond to cyber threats; and, three, working with other agencies to facilitate law enforcement and technical cooperation and provide capacity building so other countries can better work with us.

On a policy level, one of the most important issues is avoiding cyber conflict by building a global consensus on a framework for long-term cyber stability. My former office spearheaded this frame comprised of the application of international law to cyberspace, acceptance of voluntary norms of state behavior, and implementation of confidence building measures. It also includes working with the private sector in civil society on these issues. For example, the Global Commission that I serve on recently proposed a new multistakeholder developed norm, entitled "A Call to Protect the Public Core of the Internet."

U.S. work on stability is also the foundation of using diplomatic and other tools and partnerships to better deter bad actors. Norms of behaviors are irrelevant if there are no consequences for those who violate those norms. For example, the lack of a sufficiently strong, timely, and continuing response to Russian interference with our electoral process virtually guarantees that they will attempt to interfere again, both in the U.S. and other democracies around the world. We must do better.

And finally, cyber diplomacy involves promoting core values, such as Internet freedom and fair market access.

My former office made a great deal of progress in all these issues, but a tremendous amount of work lies ahead, and sustained high-level diplomatic leadership is required. I was, therefore, disappointed that the State Department, even if temporarily, chose to downgrade my former office and constrict its resources. This sends the wrong message to our adversaries and allies alike. For the U.S. to lead and continue to make significant progress in cyber diplomacy, organizational structure and resources are important. Accordingly, I am pleased that this committee proposed, and the House of Representatives passed, the bipartisan Cyber Diplomacy Act of 2017. Over my career, I have found that these issues have almost always been treated in a bipartisan manner, and I am very happy to see that reflected in this important legislation. The Cyber Diplomacy Act appropriately makes clear that international cyber issues are a national policy priority, it calls out the importance of norms and stability, and, importantly, the Act sets out a strong and appropriate organizational structure for these issues of the State Department.

By creating a statutory office of cyber issues with a broad scope of cross-cutting substantiative responsibilities at a high level, and reporting through a neutral cross-cutting reporting chain, they can give full voice to the important security issues as well as human rights and economic ones. Of course, as I noted, adequate resources are also important to the success of this mission, and I hope Congress will address this very important issue in the future.

Although much has been achieved over the last few years in cyber diplomacy, there is a long road ahead. Much needs to be done to continue to advance stability, norms, bolster deterrence, respond to threats, build partnerships, uphold human rights online, and advance fair economic access and prosperity.

So I thank you for your interest and support of diplomacy in cyberspace. And I thank you for the opportunity to testify today on these important and timely issues, and I look forward to your questions.

[The prepared statement of Mr. Painter follows:]

Testimony of Christopher M.E. Painter
Before the House Foreign Affairs Committee

Hearing on "U.S. Cyber Diplomacy in an Era of Growing Threats"

February 6th, 2018

Chairman Royce, Ranking Member Engel, members of the House Foreign Affairs Committee: it is a pleasure to appear before your Committee to discuss the growing technical and policy threats in cyberspace and the vital role of diplomacy in combatting those threats and shaping an international environment that promotes an open, interoperable, secure and reliable information and communications infrastructure around the globe. For over twenty-six years I have devoted my life to these issues, serving as a federal prosecutor, a senior official at the Department of Justice and the FBI, a Senior Director at the National Security Council and, most recently, as the first Coordinator for Cyber Issues at the Department of State. I have continued to work on these issues since leaving the federal government, among other things, serving as a Commissioner on the Global Commission for the Stability of Cyberspace and a Board member of the Center for Internet Security.

Over the course of my career, I have seen the technical threats in cyberspace posed by state and non-state actors dramatically increase in both sophistication and number, and have seen the potential and actual impact of those threats grow exponentially. I have also seen the rise of serious policy threats to the very nature, structure and governance of the Internet as we know it, unprecedented attempts to undermine democratic processes, and the increasing drive by repressive regimes to suppress and control online discourse and undermine Internet freedom. Given the severity of the threat and our increasing dependence on cyberspace, the U.S. and other governments around the world have moved from treating cyber policy —including cybersecurity, cybercrime, Internet governance and Internet freedom — as niche or technical issues to treating them as core issues of national security, economic policy, human rights and, ultimately, core issues of foreign policy.

It is clear that responding to cyber threats and seizing the many opportunities in cyberspace requires a whole-of-government response, leveraging the capabilities of agencies across the federal government and working with the private sector and civil society. It is also clear, given the international nature of the threats and the technology itself, that the State Department should play a leading role in that effort and that effective cyber diplomacy — perhaps one of the most challenging and complicated foreign policy issues facing us today — is paramount. The United States has provided significant leadership in this area in the past. Indeed, my former office, the Office of the Coordinator for Cyber Issues — the first of its kind anywhere in the world — literally created and advanced a whole new area of foreign policy focus that simply did not exist before and made substantial progress on a number of policy and operational fronts. As a testament to our leadership, and as a refection that this set of issues has come of age as an international policy priority, over twenty-five countries (including Russia and

China) have followed our example by establishing high level positions in their foreign ministries to spearhead cyber diplomacy.

For the U.S. to continue to lead, as it must, cyber issues must be re-prioritized and appropriately resourced at the State Department. Moreover, it is important that the position of the individual leading these efforts be at a very high-level — not buried in the bureaucracy or reporting through any one functionally or perspective limited chain of command. This is particularly important given the cross-cutting and interrelated nature of cyberspace issues that span a broad gamut — including national security, criminal, counter-terrorism, economic and human rights matters. This is not the time to demote these issues or step back from the world stage and cede leadership to others. That is an invitation for our adversaries to exploit our absence. Rather, given the rising tide of challenges we face in cyberspace, now is the time to elevate these issues and strengthen our country's ability to build alliances and continue to lead.

Threats in Cyberspace

A wide range of cyber intrusions and attacks directed at our government, businesses, citizens, and even the core of our democracy itself, have become a daily fixture of our lives. Threat actors are also diverse, including nation states, cybercriminals (both transnational organized groups and individuals) and terrorists, with an increased blurring of the lines between these actors especially when criminals act either at the behest, or with the tacit permission, of nation states. Recent events like the WannaCry ransomware worm illustrate emerging new destructive threats and the involvement of rouge state actors. Poorly or unsecured Internet of Things ("IOT") devices have led to new and powerful botnets and, while IoT holds incredible promise for huge economic and technological advancements, potential security issues could lead to significant harm and injury.

State-sponsored cyber intrusions and theft of information continue to be an economic and national security challenge and state-sponsored attacks pose a significant threat to both U.S. and international security. The Director of National Intelligence in his Worldwide Threat Assessment stated: "Our adversaries are becoming more adept at using cyberspace to threaten our interests and advance their own, and despite improving cyber defenses, nearly all information, communication networks and systems will be at risk for years." Like his predecessors, he listed Russia, China, Iran and North Korea as key state threats to the U.S. and terrorists and criminals as non-state threats. Over the past few years, malicious actors have used cyber means to damage and disrupt critical infrastructure and other networks, making a long time fear of such attacks a reality. And, while the U.S. has long focused on potential state sponsored attacks on critical infrastructure and the damage caused by the wide-spread theft of commercial information by state actors, it did not foresee the hybrid threat posed by Russia's cyber enabled attempt to undermine and influence the 2016 election that goes to the core of our democracy. This last challenge has played itself out in several other democracies and will be a significant issue in future U.S. elections. In addition, an increasing number of countries are developing cyber offensive capabilities with no clear doctrine for their use, raising the specter of cyber conflict, inadvertent escalation and unanticipated consequences and damage if and when they are used.

All of these challenges are exacerbated by the lack of effective deterrence and appropriate consequences for bad actors in cyberspace.

Criminals and criminal groups are becoming ever more sophisticated and creative in using cyber tools for theft, extortion (including an increase in the use of ransomware) and disruption, as well as using cyber capabilities and networks (including the Dark web) to facilitate both cyber and non-cyber criminal activity. Cybercriminal activity almost always has a significant international dimension — either because it is caused by geographically distributed trans-national criminal groups or because, even where the criminals and their victims are in the same country, smart criminals will route their communications and attacks through several countries to avoid detection and apprehension. Terrorist groups have long used cyberspace to plan, coordinate, inspire their followers, raise funds and recruit followers, and some have expressed interest in developing greater offensive cyber capabilities.

In addition to the above more technically focused threats, there are a number of policy threats and challenges facing the U.S. in cyberspace. Though cyberspace has proven to be a tremendous tool for economic expansion, innovation and social growth, many repressive or non-democratic regimes view the openness of the Internet as an existential threat to their control and stability. Those states try to restrict access on the Internet, use cyber tools to monitor their citizens, and champion the pre-eminence of absolute sovereignty over the free flow of information and international human rights. Moreover, they have sought to replace the current multi-stakeholder system of Internet governance and promote a system of intergovernmental control that would both stifle innovation and undermine Internet freedom and human rights. Other policy challenges include the risk of multiple, conflicting regulatory regimes related to various aspects of cyberspace and the Internet. For example, multiple jurisdictions are considering some sort of regulatory regime involving the Internet of Things. Forced data localization and cybersecurity regulatory regimes that appear to be more focused on "indigenous innovation" and market protectionism rather than security pose additional economic and security challenges for the U.S.

The Role of Diplomacy

Against this sobering backdrop, the need for diplomacy, working in conjunction with other instruments of our national power, is clear. Because cyberspace threats are almost always international, as is the technology itself, an unprecedented level of international coordination, engagement and cooperation is required both to counter those threats and embrace and drive the economic and social opportunities that cyberspace offers for the future. This diplomatic effort must also be cross-cutting because security, economic and human rights issues in cyberspace are often interdependent. In recognition of the need to increase our focus and leadership on international cyber issues, my former office at the State Department was created in the Secretary's Office. The office led on a number of policy and operational issues and coordinated with other offices throughout the building and the interagency on others. Some of the key areas of diplomacy in cyberspace include:

Building Strategic Partnerships and Engaging Multilaterally

A foundational aspect of cyber diplomacy is building strategic partnerships with other countries around the world to enhance collective action and cooperation against shared threats, assemble like minded coalitions on vital policy issues, share information and national initiatives and to confront bad actors. Over the course of six years, my former office established numerous senior bi-lateral and multi-lateral partnerships and launched numerous "whole of government" cyber dialogues with countries around the world. These include, among many others, Japan, Korea, Germany, France, India, the Nordic and Baltic countries, Brazil, Argentina, Israel, Mexico, Canada, Australia, the UK, New Zealand, Estonia and the EU. These formal and informal dialogues discussed the full range of cyber issues and have resulted in joint statements and, in the case of India, a comprehensive cyber framework. More importantly, they have translated into direct cooperation and common approaches in important multilateral venues. As we seek to advance common values, push back on repressive regimes and look to enhance collective action and deterrence, these partnerships need to be strengthened and expanded.

Nearly every formal and informal multilateral and regional body is now, in some capacity, focusing on cyber issues. These include multiple parts of the United Nations (including the ITU and UNODC), the Organization for Security and Cooperation in Europe ("OSCE"), APEC, ASEAN, the OAS, the G7 and the G20. While these venues offer the opportunity for the U.S. and its partners to advance a common vision of cyberspace or implement important initiatives (as we have, for example, in the OSCE on Cyber Confidence Building Measures), they also pose a challenge when non-democratic countries try to use those organizations to advance their own very different view of cyberspace. So far, working with our partners, the private sector, and civil society, we have generally been successful in advancing our agenda of an open and secure cyberspace and thwarting attempts by repressive regimes to impose state control over the Internet or undermine security or human rights. However, I believe we are at an inflection point, where the debates and decisions made in these forums over the next several years will have a major impact on all of these issues. If we are to advance our vision and defend our core values, the U.S. must continue to engage at a senior level in these many forums.

Enhancing Cooperation, Collective Action, Incident Response and Capacity Building

Diplomacy and diplomatic tools play an important role in directly responding to cyber threats and laying the groundwork for better cooperation and action against future threats. For example, using the network of counterparts we had built with other countries, my former office used diplomatic demarches to seek the assistance of over twenty countries when a persistent Iranian sponsored botnet was targeting U.S. financial institutions. This collective action, where each country used its authorities and tools to help address a shared threat, proved very effective in mitigating the malicious activity. Longer term and high level diplomatic pressure played a key role in addressing widespread trade secret and intellectual property theft by China. This included both working with other countries who were also victimized and a sustained campaign of direct diplomatic engagement by the U.S. This diplomatic campaign helped lead to the negotiation of a landmark agreement with China that made clear that no country should use cyber means to steal the intellectual property of another to benefit its commercial sector. Diplomacy and the State Department also have a vital role in working with DOJ and DHS to facilitate law enforcement and technical cooperation. Part of this facilitation is incident specific and part is working with countries to enhance their capabilities so that they can better work with us to combat threats. For example, my former office worked closely with DOJ to expand the countries who are members of the Budapest Convention on Cybercrime and with DHS in helping countries establish Computer Security Incident Response Teams.

Capacity Building also is important both to enabling better cooperation and in persuading other countries that our vision of cyberspace benefits and should be endorsed by them. My former office worked extensively with DOJ, DHS and others to create and implement ambitious cost-effective capacity building initiatives. These initiatives helped developing countries enhance cybercrime fighting capacity, create national cyber strategies and help create institutional and other mechanisms to protect against cyber threats that, given the global nature of these threats, allow them to not only protect their own networks but assist in the security of ours. We also worked with countries as they developed their cybersecurity policies to ensure that they properly accounted for human rights and economic access concerns. While modest amounts of funding for capacity building pay comparatively large dividends, both in bolstering our own security and in promoting U.S. leadership, unfortunately, funding for these efforts has been dramatically curtailed.

Advancing Strategic Policy and Building a Consensus for Global Cyber Stability

A cornerstone of U.S. cyber diplomacy is promoting and protecting core values such as openness, Internet freedom and multi-stakeholder Internet governance that have all been threatened over the last several years. The U.S. is a founding member of the Freedom Online Coalition and has raised Internet freedom and Internet governance issues in virtually every diplomatic engagement. Diplomacy must also be used to push back on flawed cyber regulatory regimes or policies that serve to fragment the Internet and risk undermining its incredible social and economic potential. We have used diplomatic channels to challenge forced data localization regimes, ill-conceived cyber regulatory approaches and market access restrictions, and have partnered with the Department of Commerce in promoting the NIST Cybersecurity Framework with partners around the world. And, diplomacy plays a vital role in ensuring the long term stability of cyberspace itself in the face of increasing nation state and other threats, so that everyone can enjoy the benefits of cyberspace and so no state has an incentive to engage in disruptive behavior. Though all of these are of these are important issues, all requiring substantial diplomatic international engagement, in the interest of time, I will focus on the last.

As countries around the globe are developing, and in some cases using, cyber offensive and other capabilities, the lack of any clear consensus on acceptable state behavior in cyberspace poses substantial risks to the many benefits it offers. To address this, the U.S. has led the development and promotion of a strategic framework of cyber stability that includes (1) global affirmation of the applicability of international law to state activity in cyberspace; (2) the development of voluntary, non-binding peacetime norms of acceptable state behavior; and (3) the development and use of practical confidence building measures (CBMs) that serve to reduce the risk of misperception and escalation in cyberspace. The U.S., led by my former office, has had great success in promoting and achieving acceptance of this framework in forums around the world including in the Group of Governmental Experts (UN GGE) on international cyber security (a series of expert forums in the United Nations), NATO and the Organization for Security and Cooperation in Europe. In the 2013 UN GGE report, countries, including the U.S., China and Russia, reached a landmark consensus that international law, including the U.N. Charter, applies in cyberspace. That means that cyberspace is not a "free fire" zone where no rules apply but is grounded in the same rules as the physical world. In 2015, the UN GGE recommended voluntary, norms of responsible state behavior including several peacetime norms that the U.S. has advocated. These voluntary, non-binding norms included states refraining from attacking the critical infrastructure of another state, states refraining from attacking Computer Security Incident Response Teams, and states cooperating with requests for assistance in certain cyber attacks. The agreement on a theft of trade secret norm that the U.S. reached with China was adopted by the G20 and by other country bi-lateral agreements with China. The U.S. also made substantial progress in the OSCE in taking forward and implementing cyber CBMs.

While all of this represents significant progress in achieving global cyber stability, there is much more to be done and the head winds are stiff. The 2016 UN GGE ended in a stalemate, some authoritarian regimes are aggressively promoting their own vision of cyberspace that restricts openness, and some regimes are resisting necessary efforts to assess exactly how international law applies to cyberspace. There is an urgent need to build a broader consensus among countries on the norms we have put forth, much work required to implement them, and significant effort ahead on further articulating how international law applies to cyberspace. This again will require a sustained high level and well resourced effort by the State Department not only with large multilateral organizations, but also with smaller groups of countries and in regional venues.

Of course, discussion of norms and cyber stability are not just the province of governments — though governments are in a unique position to implement them. There has been great work done in thinking through these issues by the private sector and civil society. I currently serve as a Commissioner on the Global Commission for the Stability of Cyberspace, an international initiative that was formed to help foster stability and advance a global multi stakeholder engagement on these issues. That group recently proposed a Call to Protect the Public Core of the Internet. It is an appeal for a new global norm to apply to both state and non-state actors to refrain from activity that intentionally and substantially damages the general accessibility or integrity of the Internet itself. The Commission is engaging with governments and other stakeholders on this proposed norm now and is considering other cyber stability measures to be proposed in the future. Other companies and organizations are active and have performed good work in this area as well.

Like nearly everything in cyberspace, public private partnerships are important in cyber diplomacy. Our policies are better and have a stronger chance of success when the government interacts with civil society and the private sector and it is important for the Department to work with these groups across the full range of cyber issues in a coordinated manner.

Deterrence

While the U.S. has made significant progress (with much more to do) in building an international consensus on what constitutes responsible state behavior in cyberspace, that work is largely irrelevant if there are no consequences for those who violate that consensus. We simply have not done a very good job of deterring malicious actors — particularly nation state actors. There are many reasons for this including difficulties with attribution, a limited tool set of potential consequences, and difficulties sharing information with partner countries. Nevertheless, at the heart of deterrence is the threat of a credible and timely response to the transgressor. Failure to act in a credible or timely way creates its own norm of inaction and signals to the adversary that their actions are acceptable — or at the very least cost free. For example, the lack a sufficiently strong, timely and continuing response to Russian interference with our electoral process virtually guarantees that they will attempt to interfere again, both in the U.S. and in other democratic countries. We must do better.

Diplomacy can and should play a vital role in this effort. Diplomacy is of course one of the key tools in the tool set of response options that also include law enforcement actions, economic sanctions, cyber and kinetic responses. We must continue to employ diplomacy effectively and work to enhance all of our existing response options. We must also work with our like-minded partners and other stakeholders to creatively develop new tools that can be imposed swiftly and be reversible in order to change an adversaries' behavior — expanding the tool set and communicating, as transparently as possible, the likely costs that will be imposed for bad behavior. And, we must enhance collective action. Although the U.S. always reserves the option to act alone if it must, deterrence and legitimacy is better served when several countries band together against a bad actor. There is much diplomatic work to do in forming such an agile coalition of like-minded countries who can call out bad behavior and collectively impose costs on our adversaries. Such a coalition should flexible and can involve different countries and different actions depending on the actor, but creating it, and solving information sharing and other issues, will require a significant diplomatic effort.

Incorporating Foreign Policy Concerns into Broader Policy and Operational Decisions

Foreign policy considerations also play an important role in sensitive operational, military, law enforcement and other decisions and policies related to cyberspace and technology. It is vital for the State Department to have a senior voice at the interagency table for this range of issues to ensure that our actions and policies fully account for potential foreign policy concerns and to make sure we are pursuing the most effective course.

Creating an Effective Structure for Cyber Diplomacy

Although I have only briefly touched on the many areas of critical cyber policy in my discussion today, it is abundantly clear that diplomacy plays an indispensable role in keeping our country safe, promoting global cyber stability and promoting and defending economic interests and human rights in the digital world. It is also clear that there is a tremendous amount of work to be done and that senior, sustained and cross-cutting diplomatic leadership is imperative. Given the centrality and growing importance of these issues, and the leadership role the U.S. and the State Department had established, it was unfortunate that the Department chose to essentially eliminate my former position, downgrade these issues to a lower level, and fold my former office into an ill-fitting and overly narrow reporting chain that has a primary focuses on economic issues alone. Regardless of the qualifications or title of the person who takes on this portfolio, there is a huge difference, both within the Department and in dealing with interagency and foreign counterparts, between reporting to the Secretary (working with the Deputy, Under Secretaries and Assistant Secretaries across the Department), and being placed several rungs down the ladder reporting to a singe functionally focused Assistant Secretary. That organizational structure also hampers the ability to coordinate across the many important cyber issues that I have discussed today— including core security and human rights matters — that don't fit within a single functional mandate. Indeed, while economic issues are very important, everyone is to some extent a prisoner of their perspective, and its hard to see how issues around sensitive cyber operations, deterrence, norms of state behavior, fighting cybercrime, terrorist use of the Internet, responding to significant cyber incidents or even Internet freedom issues can be given full voice and consideration in that setting. Even if this organizational structure for cyber issues is only temporary, as was stated by the Deputy Secretary several months ago, it sends the wrong message to our adversaries, who seek to exploit any perceived lack of U.S. leadership, and to our allies, who are left to wonder about our continuing commitment.

For the U.S to lead and continue to make significant progress on cyber diplomacy, organizational structure and resources are important. The position leading these efforts must be high-level, with broad cross-cutting and coordinating authority and it must report through a neutral reporting chain that allows full consideration of the broad range of issues in cyberspace. Of course, especially as cyber issues continue to gain prominence and are intertwined with physical world issues, other functional offices and their expertise will have an important role to play, and not every issue involving cyberspace or the Internet needs to be placed fully in one office. However, an effective cyber office and the person leading it needs to have clear coordinating authority over the broad range of cyber issues throughout the Department. Given the enormity and increasing importance of its mission, such an office also needs robust personnel, operating and capacity building (foreign assistance) resources. Over a six year period, I worked to build a well staffed and resourced office that, even at its height, was struggling to keep up with the constant and increasing demands of the dynamic cyber portfolio. Now, because of the hiring freeze, cost cutting and potential reorganization, I understand that my former office is operating at a significantly reduced strength, and that its foreign assistance budget has been virtually zeroed out. Finally, for cyber diplomacy to succeed, these issues need to be a real and publicly stated priority for the Secretary, and the person leading these efforts should have access to the Secretary and Deputy Secretary when needed.

The Cyber Diplomacy Act of 2017

Accordingly, I am pleased that this Committee proposed, and the House of Representatives passed, the bi-partisan Cyber Diplomacy Act of 2017. Over my lengthy career, I have found that these issues have almost always been treated in a bi-partisan manner and I am happy to see that reflected in this important legislation. The Cyber Diplomacy Act appropriately makes clear that international cyber issues and cyber diplomacy are a national policy priority. The "findings" section of the Act and the section on implementation reflect the broad range of cyber issues in play and gives appropriate emphasis to security, human rights and economic issues. It also appropriately recognizes the importance of cyber stability and responsible norms of state behavior in cyberspace.

Importantly, the Act sets out a strong and appropriate organizational structure for these issues at the State Department. First, it creates, by statute, the Office of Cyber Issues — giving needed permanence to this vital mission. Second, it articulates that the Office and the person heading it should have appropriately broad cross-cutting substantive duties — including leading diplomatic cyberspace efforts "relating to international cybersecurity, internet access, internet freedom, digital economy, cybercrime, deterrence and international responses to cyber threats" and coordinating within the State Department and the interagency cyberspace efforts and other relevant functions. Third, it specifically calls out the need for the position to work with the public and private sector on cyberspace issues. And, fourth, it makes clear that the head of the Office is to be "the principal cyber-policy official within the senior management of the Department of State and advisor to the Secretary of State for cyber issues."

The Act also helpfully prescribes that the head of the Office shall have an ambassadorial rank and be Senate confirmed. While this is important and appropriate given the importance of these issues — and helps with signaling to other governments and for accountability — I believe sufficiently high-level placement within the State Department hierarchy is of at least equal, if not even greater importance. For, example, a Deputy Assistant Secretary, even of ambassadorial rank, does not cary the same clout in the Department, with other governments or with other agencies, or the same access to the Secretary, as someone with an Assistant Secretary or equivalent position. That is especially true because a Deputy Assistant Secretary must normally report through an Assistant Secretary who will almost certainly have a more narrow functional or regional purview. Ideally, given the cross-cutting nature of the issues and the value of signaling the importance and authority of the position both to foreign governments and to interagency colleagues, the official should report directly to the Secretary, as I did, or the Deputy Secretary. The Act does not exclude that possibility, stating instead that the "head of the Office shall report to the Undersecretary of Political Affairs or official holding a higher position at the Department of State." Given, the current reticence to create or maintain additional direct reports to the Secretary, this is a fair compromise. Currently, the only more senior officials at State than the Political Undersecretary, are the Secretary and Deputy Secretary. Also, the Political Undersecretary, who has jurisdiction over all the regional bureaus, provides a neutral reporting chain and a broad perspective that is not stove-piped within any single functional perspective. Moreover, the Political Undersecretary can help with mainstreaming cyber issues throughout the Department and, most importantly, within the regional bureaus and our posts around the world. While I was at State, I worked with the Political Undersecretary who tasked each of the regional assistant secretaries to create comprehensive regional cyber strategies. These strategies not only helped raise the importance of these issues throughout the Department, but also were key building blocks for implementing our programs, working with our posts, and training a cadre of cyber officers in the field. As for level, presumably a direct report to the Political Undersecretary would be cast as an Assistant Secretary equivalent. Moreover, the Act helpfully notes that nothing in the Act prevents the office from being elevated to a full Bureau or the head from being officially designated as an Assistant Secretary — indeed, the Act contains a sense of Congress that this should happen.

The Cyber Diplomacy Act goes a long way toward addressing the urgent international cyber policy issues facing our country, and addressing the structure we need at the State Department to maintain and advance our leadership role. Of course, as I have noted, this effort must also be prioritized in terms of resources and I hope Congress will address this important issue in the future.

<u>Conclusion and Way Forward</u>

Although much has been achieved over the last few years in cyber diplomacy, we are still at the beginning of this journey and there is a long road ahead. The work and the choices we make now and over the next few years will determine whether we can all benefit from this amazing technology, or whether both growing policy and technical threats will undermine its incredible potential. Achieving the future we want will require continued high level attention and a significant, sustained, effort. Diplomacy has and must continue to play a pivotal role — shaping the environment, building cooperation, and working to build coalitions to respond to shared threats — and we must continue to lead the international community. I have only briefly touched on in my testimony the enormity of the work ahead. Much needs to be done to continue to advance stability and norms, bolster deterrence, respond to threats, build partnerships, uphold human rights online, and advance fair economic access and prosperity. Much more needs to be done as well to deal with existing and future hybrid threats — including combined cyber/ influence operation threats that attempt to undermine our democracy. Cyber Diplomacy is the quintessential 21st century issue of our foreign policy — involving aspects of human rights, security and economic policy. It requires cross-cutting leadership that leverages all of our capabilities, across the government, with the private sector and civil society, and with our foreign partners.

Thank you for the opportunity to testify today on this important and timely issue, and thank you for your interest and support for diplomacy in cyberspace. I look forward to your questions.

Chairman ROYCE. Mr. Miller.

STATEMENT OF MR. JOHN MILLER, VICE PRESIDENT FOR GLOBAL POLICY AND LAW, CYBERSECURITY, AND PRIVACY, INFORMATION TECHNOLOGY INDUSTRY COUNCIL

Mr. MILLER. Chairman Royce, Ranking Member Engel, and distinguished members of the committee, on behalf of the Information Technology Industry Council, or ITI, thank you for the opportunity to testify today regarding the importance of U.S. cyber diplomacy in a world of growing threats.

ITI is a global policy advocacy organization representing over 60 leading technology and innovation companies from all corners of the tech sector and beyond, all doing business globally.

As we survey the global the cyber policy landscape, we see a remarkable level of activity signifying both opportunity and risk. A central element of ITI's global advocacy efforts involves helping governments understand the critical importance of cross-border data flows to the tech sector and the global economy. Data is central to the cutting-edge technologies and innovations that continue to extend the benefits of the Internet, including cloud computing, the Internet of Things, big data analytics, and artificial intelligence.

The ability to freely move data across borders is essential, not only to every business that operates internationally, but also to our ability to do everything from securing global networks and the personal data of customers to conducting international trade.

Unfortunately, policymakers globally are responding to the expanding sophistication and capabilities of cyber adversaries, as well as more frequent and severe cyber incidents, by building virtual cyber policy walls at their borders, by proposing cyber laws and policies that threaten to impede cross-border data flows, create trade barriers for U.S. companies, and undermine the trust and interoperability necessary for the global digital economy to continue to thrive.

The trends we are most concerned about fall into four categories: One, forced localization, which refers to a broad set of policies designed to compel companies to relocate all or part of their business operations within a country's borders, including storing or processing data on servers or data centers located in-country as a precondition for market access; two, siloed or country-specific standards and regulations, such as privacy-based transfer restrictions, or security-based testing requirements which pose significant risk to interoperability and data flows; three, efforts by policymakers to impose cybersecurity audit assessment and testing requirements on private entities, a potentially invasive practice that contemplates testing conducted by government auditors, often requiring access to companies' intellectual property; and four, the application of legacy regulations to technology and services innovations.

Two recent examples of this rising trend include subjecting U.S. online services to so-called over-the-top regulations, and expanding use of export controls, most notably in the context of innovative cybersecurity technologies.

It is also important to understand that our global cyber policy threats aren't isolated to a few countries, regions, or economies;

they are everywhere. It has been well-documented that some countries, such as China and Russia, are taking approaches that incorporate many of these troubling cyber policy trends. But it is also critical to understand that policymakers in major economies, including the European Union, India, Brazil, and many others, are pursuing similar policies.

Now for the good news. On balance, recent cyber policy activity in the U.S. embraces an approach that furthers global data flows, interoperability, innovation, and trust, avoiding many of these policy pitfalls. The Cyber Diplomacy Act of 2017 recounts many of these cyber policy achievements, as did Mr. Painter. And to that list, we would add the Cybersecurity Threat Information Sharing Act passed by Congress in 2016, as well as the cybersecurity framework, a voluntary risk management-based framework grounded in international standards and best practices.

The Cyber Diplomacy Act will complement these efforts well and provides a great encapsulation of the types of international cyber policy approaches needed to support an open, interoperable, and secure Internet that promotes data flows, innovation, and economic prosperity. The bill provides a roadmap for how the U.S. Government can translate this expression of policy into action, including by securing and implementing commitments based on accepted cyber policy norms, holding the counter parties to those agreements accountable for their implementation, and prioritizing and resourcing the State Department's cyber function to maximize success.

To complement the Cyber Diplomacy Act's solid foundation, we offer three additional recommendations designed to help the U.S. Government maintain its leadership position in cyberspace, while avoiding the potential that China's cybersecurity law emerges as the dominant approach to cyber policy in the region, or even globally.

First, to counter the trend of various countries increasingly advocating for their own local standards, testing protocols, and certifications, the U.S. needs a proactive and adequately resourced national cyber standardization strategy.

Second, promoting the cybersecurity framework approach internationally as a counterweight to the data-restrictive policy approaches gaining prominence globally can help the U.S. sustain its leadership position on cybersecurity policy around the world.

And third, pursuing multilateral solutions in parallel with bilateral agreements can be an important force multiplier to drive scalable policy solutions across the digital economy.

We look forward to the opportunity to continue to work with Congress and the administration on this important set of issues. Thank you, again, for the opportunity to share our perspective, and I look forward to your questions.

[The prepared statement of Mr. Miller follows:]

Written Testimony of

John S. Miller
Vice President for Global Policy and Law
Cybersecurity and Privacy
Information Technology Industry Council (ITI)

Before the

Committee on Foreign Affairs

U.S. House of Representatives

U.S. Cyber Diplomacy in an Era of Growing Threats

February 6, 2018

Written Testimony of
John S. Miller
Vice President for Global Policy and Law, Cybersecurity and Privacy
Information Technology Industry Council (ITI)

Before the
Committee on Foreign Affairs
U.S. House of Representatives

U.S. Cyber Diplomacy in an Era of Growing Threats

February 6, 2018

Chairman Royce, Ranking Member Engel, and Distinguished Members of the Committee on Foreign Affairs, thank you for the opportunity to testify today. I am John Miller, Vice President for Global Policy and Law, Cybersecurity and Privacy at the Information Technology Industry Council (ITI), and I am pleased to testify before your committee today on the important topic of assessing U.S. cyber diplomacy, including the State Department's cyber functions, in an era of growing threats. As we survey the global cyber policy landscape, we agree we are living in a time of remarkable global cyber policy activity, signifying both opportunity and risk. While it's instructive to understand where the policy landmines representing those risks are currently located and how they can undermine the United States government's (USG's) cyber policy objectives, global cybersecurity efforts, and the competitiveness of U.S. companies, it's also important for us to seize the opportunity presented by this global uncertainty to advance cyber policies that promote the cross-border data flows underpinning competitiveness, economic growth, and security. We welcome your interest and engagement on this subject.

ITI[1] represents over 60[2] of the world's leading information and communications technology (ICT) companies. Cybersecurity and cyber policy more broadly are rightly a priority for governments and our industry, and we share common goals of improving cybersecurity, protecting the privacy of individuals' data, and maintaining strong intellectual property protections. Further, our members are global companies, doing business in countries around the world. Most service the global market via complex supply chains in which products are developed, made, and assembled in multiple countries, and service customers across the full range of global industry sectors, such as financial services, healthcare and energy. We thus acutely understand the impact of governments' policies on innovation and the need for U.S. policies to be compatible with – and drive – global norms, as well as the potential impacts on our customers. Our members have extensive experience working with governments around the world

---

[1] **About ITI.** ITI is the global voice of the tech sector. We advocate for global public policies that advance innovation; open access to new and emerging markets; promote e-commerce expansion; drive sustainability and efficiency; protect consumer choice and privacy, and enable the transformational economic, societal, and commercial opportunities that our companies are creating. ITI's members comprise leading technology and innovation companies from all corners of the ICT sector, including hardware, software, digital services, semiconductor, network equipment, cybersecurity, internet companies, and companies using technology to fundamentally evolve their businesses. ITI's diverse membership and expert staff provide a broad perspective and intelligent insight in confronting the implications and opportunities of policy activities around the world. Visit http://www.iti.org/ to learn more. Follow us on Twitter for the latest ITI news @ITI_TechTweets.

[2] See ITI membership list at http://www.itic.org/about/member-companies.

on cyber or digital policies. In the technology industry, as well as other global sectors, when discussing any cyber policy, it is important to consider our connectedness, which is truly global and borderless.

Taking a global approach is at once our top priority and challenge, because policymakers don't necessarily look at these issues through the same lens as global companies – many understandably refract cybersecurity, for instance, through their sovereign rights and obligations to protect their territories and their citizens. Unfortunately, doing the equivalent of building policy walls at your borders in the name of better security doesn't work in the digital world – from either a business or technical perspective – and may have the unintended consequence of doing more harm than good.

I will focus my testimony on four areas: (1) demonstrating the critical importance and interrelatedness of cross-border data flows to the top cyber policy issues our companies grapple with every day; (2) illustrating how some of the top global cyber policy trends put global data flows, security, and our companies' competitiveness at risk; (3) positioning recent U.S. cyber policy activity within this global context; and (4) offering recommendations on the path forward, including discussing how the policies expressed in the *Cyber Diplomacy Act* (H.R. 3776) can help advance our collective cyber policy interests.

Cross-Border Data Flows and the Top Cyber Policy Issues Facing the ICT Sector

A central element of ITI's global advocacy efforts involves helping governments understand the critical importance of cross-border data flows to the ICT sector and the global economy, and the centrality of data to many cutting-edge technologies and innovations, such as the Internet of Things (IoT), Artificial Intelligence (AI) and big data analytics. Virtually every business that operates internationally relies instinctively on the free and near instantaneous movement of data across borders to enable their day-to-day business operations, from conducting research and development, to designing and manufacturing goods, to marketing and distributing products and services to their customers, to securing global networks and the personal data of customers across the globe. With data increasingly at the center of not only the global economy but our lives, securing that data, and protecting privacy of individuals' data, is of paramount importance to ITI's companies, and the data-driven innovations mentioned above are increasingly critical to our shared cybersecurity mission as well.

In addition to facilitating secure business transactions amongst companies in disparate locales, global data flows are key to greater coordination and productivity for global companies, helping to secure the systems and networks that manage production schedules and Human Resources data, as well as to communicate internally with subsidiaries and employees in different geographies. The free flow of data across borders is also necessary to enable a seamless and secure internet experience for hundreds of millions of citizens around the globe.

I suspect the top "buckets" of cyber policy issues facing ITI's companies – international trade and data flows; standards and regulations; privacy and data protection; and cybersecurity – are the same issues facing most companies doing business in the global, digital economy. And so it's not surprising that all these issues implicate data flows in one way or another.

Data Flows and International Trade. We think of these issues together, because for our companies these issues are inextricably linked. There is no trade in the modern, global digital economy without the ability to move data across borders – transferring data, communicating data, storing data, and of course protecting data are all fundamental to digital trade. Cross border data flows are fundamental to businesses of all sizes, and in all geographies, as well as to the key innovations that will drive the future,

such as IoT and AI. The value of cross border data flows to e-commerce and digital trade cannot be overstated, and indeed there are plenty of statistics we can cite placing the aggregate dollar values of cross-border data flows between the U.S. and any number of trading partners in the hundreds of billions of dollars with the overall value of such data flows involving the U.S. topping $6 trillion in 2014.[3] It is important to note these numbers are so large because the impacts involve much more than just the U.S. ICT sector – here in the U.S., or in countries proposing or adopting protectionist measures. The ICT sector is a horizontal enabler of services trade across all sectors of the economy. A recent study by UNCTAD – the United Nations Conference on Trade and Development – found up to 75% of the benefits of e-commerce impact other sectors of local economies. Misunderstanding of this fact amongst developing countries is palpable, as policies designed to "grow a domestic ICT sector" will have much broader negative impacts, as businesses in developing economies such as Brazil and India will not be able to grow and operate on a global scale without the ability to move data across borders.

Standards and Regulations. Trade associations representing global businesses are often characterized as "anti-regulation" – and of course, it's true that not a lot of businesses go out of their way to ask to have regulations imposed on them. However, when we survey emerging standards and regulations globally, the bigger problems often aren't necessarily the standards and regulations themselves, but the fact that many countries are contemplating *local* standards, and *local, siloed* regulatory approaches. The proliferation of siloed technical standards, regulations and localized data and security requirements could impede the seamless functioning of the internet and global digital economy as we experience it today. Multiple country specific standards, or requiring that non-domestically sourced equipment undergo differing security requirements, can lead to the balkanization of the global digital infrastructure, threatening the continued interoperability of the innovative technologies that have fueled the internet's growth. The potential negative impacts of forced localization and other protectionist measures become even more pronounced when we factor in potential impacts on the cloud, Big Data, IoT, and emerging technologies such as AI.

Privacy and Data Protection. We all acknowledge that exponentially more data is being generated than ever before. Unlike natural resources, data is an infinite resource because we create it, and then data itself is leveraged through a host of innovative technologies that help unlock its value. Whether we are talking about Big Data Analytics, IoT, AI – data is at the center of all these innovations. Given data is at the center of trade and innovation, securing that data, and protecting the privacy of that data, is of paramount importance to governments, companies and citizens alike, to protect consumer privacy and to enable secure transactions. Governments around the world are aware of this as well, and many are examining, re-examining, or considering privacy and data protection laws for the first time. But data protection policies that seek to protect data by, for instance, restricting its cross-border transfer by requiring a determination of whether the receiving country's laws are "adequate," or preventing data from leaving a country's borders entirely by requiring that it be stored on domestic servers, can not only prevent future innovative uses of data, but may prevent us from realizing a host of socioeconomic uses that data helps us realize , in areas such as health, agriculture, finance, and cybersecurity.

Cybersecurity. Cybersecurity is often the rationale lurking behind many of the problematic policies that threaten data flows, such as data localization policies, proposed requirements for in-country security

---

[3] See *Digital Globalization: The New Era of Global Flows*, McKinsey Global Institute, March 2016, available at https://www.mckinsey.com/~/media/McKinsey/Business%20Functions/McKinsey%20Digital/Our%20Insights/Digital%20globali zation%20The%20new%20era%20of%20global%20flows/MGI-Digital-globalization-Full-report.ashx

testing, audits or assessments, or requirements for domestic manufacturing or server locations. The net result of such policies will likely be a slowing or diminishing of cross border data flows, which will in turn negatively impact global e-commerce development and growth. However, what is sometimes overlooked is that data flows are of central importance to cybersecurity itself. U.S. and global ICT companies have a long history of exchanging security-related information across borders with geographically-dispersed employees, users, customers, governments, and other stakeholders, which helps them better protect their own systems and maintain high levels of security for customer data, IP and the technology ecosystem as a whole. Indeed, one of the preeminent cyber policy achievements in the U.S. in recent years – the 2016 passage of a bipartisan cybersecurity threat information sharing legislation[4] – was intended to spur the voluntary sharing of cyber threat information among and between businesses and government entities to improve cybersecurity. So, it's critical to understand that the trend of impeding data flows generally is also contrary to the thrust of current U.S. cybersecurity policy and threatens to undermine progress to better secure the global digital ecosystem and economy.

Top Global Cyber Policy Trends

The policy issues described above manifest themselves in various global cyber policy trends, sometimes alone but oftentimes in combination. After briefly discussing these trends, I will highlight the current state of play in a few major economies to help illustrate the pervasiveness of today's "global policy threats."

Forced Localization. Forced localization refers to a broad set of policies that are designed to compel companies to relocate all or part of their global business operations within a country's borders. Data localization is a prime example: foreign firms could be required to process data at a national datacenter, purchase or manufacture locally, or transfer intellectual property to a domestic competitor as a precondition for market access. We've seen localization proposals popping up almost everywhere over the last few years – and while such measures today have become increasingly complex, often they are designed to achieve a straightforward goal: impeding the ability of foreign companies to compete with local firms in providing goods, services, and technologies in global business transactions. While many governments view these policies as helping them to meet the challenges of a complex global economy, the truth is the drawbacks for a country and its citizens far outweigh the benefits. Instead, localization efforts work to reduce the competitiveness of countries who employ them across all economic sectors and undermine the health of the global economy by raising the cost of doing business internationally.

While much of the discussion of forced localization policies has appropriately focused on data localization, in fact forced localization policies can take many forms, including:

- *Data Localization*: Requirements that companies store, process, or otherwise handle data within a country's borders. This includes restrictions on the free flow of information across borders that underpins an open internet.
- *Local Content Requirements*: Mandates that a certain amount of the final value of a good or service be sourced domestically, either by purchasing it from local companies or by manufacturing or otherwise producing or providing it locally.

---

[4] *Cybersecurity Information Sharing Act of 2015*

- *Technology Transfer Requirements*: Measures requiring businesses to transfer proprietary intellectual property directly to local competitors or through government agencies.
- *Local Presence Requirements*: Requiring a company to establish a local office in-country or provide goods or services using local facilities, infrastructure, or agents, etc.
- *Standards and Conformity Assessment*: Requirements to comply with unique, non-global technical standards, or to conduct duplicative or overly restrictive conformity assessment procedures without recognition of international norms that make current technology and new innovations possible.
- *Indigenous Innovation Requirements*: Requirements to use or impose a preference to domestically developed technology.
- *Domestic Employment Requirements*: Requirements to achieve a certain level of domestic employment.

The proliferation of forced localization measures is a trend that the world's leading economies – including the U.S. – - must work hard to combat if policymakers want to continue to leverage the internet to spur innovation, job creation, and economic growth. Given that localization policies are out of step with the international norms and policy frameworks that have guided innovation in technologies and the rapid rise of technology-enabled industries, the rise of such policies in recent years should be cause for concern.

ITI has conducted an in-depth survey of forced localization policies worldwide. While half of localization measures are acknowledged by governments as having a naked economic objective, such as local ICT sector development, in nearly half of the cases ITI has studied there are noneconomic rationales or objectives, often security-related, lurking behind these policies.[5]

There is a certain irony in security being cited as a driving rationale in roughly one-third of the forced localization cases ITI studied – such policies may negatively impact security itself. As noted above, there is a security rationale underlying many of the proposed localization regulations, and few would question the sovereign right of nations to pursue cybersecurity or other regulations that will legitimately protect their national security. However, in our view many of these proposed security requirements, while well intentioned, are grounded in a fundamental misconception – that location of manufacture or the country of origin of an IT product is somehow dispositive of the security of that product, or that the location of data or restricting its flow guarantees stronger protections.

In fact, geographic-based restrictions are simply not a reliable way to create better security. Fundamentally, product security is a function of how a product is made, used, and maintained, not by whom or where such products are made. Geographic-based restrictions not only ignore the reality that most supply chains for IT products are global, but run the risk of creating a false sense of security for any countries who advocate for such provisions to advance their national cybersecurity interests. At a time when greater global cooperation and collaboration is essential to improve cybersecurity, restrictions

---

[5] ITI's 2015 research indicated security-related objectives behind roughly one-third of forced localization laws, with national security cited as the primary objective 22% of the time, and government access to data for law enforcement or national security purposes cited 9 % of the time. Privacy/data protection was the stated objective behind governments' forced localization policies in an additional 13% of the cases we studied. So, while relatively transparent protectionism is clearly driving a good chunk of these problematic laws, the full picture complicated by noneconomic factors such as security and privacy.

based solely on geography risk undermining the advancement of global best practices and consensus-based standards for cybersecurity, such as secure development lifecycles.

Siloed or Country-specific Standards and Regulations. Countries are increasingly proposing regulations or standards that are country specific, rather than grounded in international standards or approaches – whether we are talking about privacy-based transfer restrictions or security-based testing requirements. Different requirements across countries pose significant regulatory fragmentation risks. The negative impacts of regulatory fragmentation include the inefficiencies associated with companies potentially being required to adopt a separate privacy and security compliance program for every country they do business in, and pose significant challenges to global interoperability due to varying technical or legal requirements. Layer on top of that sector specific laws within these countries, competing overlapping regulations (e.g., competing security incident notification and data breach notification), or multiple levels of government regulators potentially getting into the mix (e.g., Brazil's financial regulator promulgating security regulations for banks), and it's easy to see the potential problems in this area.

Cybersecurity Audits, Assessments and Testing Requirements. Efforts by policymakers to "measure," "certify," "test" or "label" for cybersecurity – e.g., the EU's proposed ENISA Regulation urging the development of a security certification Framework, or India's Department of Telecommunications proposed implementation of local security certification and testing requirements for telecommunications equipment – show no signs of abating. While these and other policy proposals are wide ranging, at their core is a common set of underlying concerns regarding the trustworthiness and security of ICT products, supply chains and systems. While determining how best to use cybersecurity measurements to drive increased accountability for cybersecurity across organizations is unquestionably a worthwhile goal, global proposals seeking to impose certification, audit or assessment requirements on private entities are often invasive in that they contemplate such tests being conducted by government auditors or assessors, thus requiring access to companies' source code or other proprietary information. Further, the testing contemplated often involves local standards, rather than global standards. A better approach to driving accountability via measurement is espoused by Draft 2 of Cybersecurity Framework Version 1.1, which emphasizes the role of measurement as a tool for self-assessment and internal use by organizations, rather than as intended for external use by policymakers or regulators to evaluate or judge the sufficiency of organizations' cybersecurity risk management programs.

Application of Legacy Regulations to Technology and Services Innovations. Of emerging concern are the attempts to "retrofit" legacy regulations to technology and services innovations in a manner that that would impact broad swaths of the internet economy, or have unintended consequences on innovation, security, or other dimensions of cyber policy. Two recent examples of this trend involve the rise of "OTT" regulations, and the expanding use of export controls.

The Rise of "OTT" Regulations. Numerous foreign governments are seeking to subject U.S. online services and applications to burdensome legacy regulations designed to address the particular technical and market characteristics of traditional telecommunications or broadcast providers. These measures – often vaguely called "Over-the-Top" or "OTT" regulations in foreign markets – take different forms globally. What they increasingly require is that online services register as telecommunications or broadcasting providers, contribute to universal service funds, comply with local content quotas and

make subsidy payments, guarantee a particular quality of service, establish local presence and/or local data storage, and implement technical mandates, including certain emergency calling requirements that are not technically feasible or economically reasonable. These regulations are creating market access barriers for U.S. services, including in China, Colombia, the European Union and several EU member states, Ghana, India, Indonesia, Kenya, Thailand, United Arab Emirates, Vietnam, and other countries.

Extension of Export Controls to Cybersecurity Products. Another troubling regulatory trend that appears on the rise is the extension of export controls to cybersecurity technologies. During the 2013 Wassenaar Arrangement plenary session, the member nations agreed to implement export controls related to intrusion detection software and IP network communications surveillance items. While the human rights concerns underlying the controls were laudable (i.e., protecting activists from monitoring by authoritarian governments and keeping software and technology out of the hands of hackers who could use it maliciously), the controls as originally agreed to were overbroad, sweeping in virtually any type of software, hardware, and technology designed to counter "intrusion" software. The 2013 controls were also ineffective in achieving their intended objective of barring companies from exporting specific tools to specific end-users for specific purposes, were divergently applied across Wassenaar signatories, and from the perspective of most would have undermined U.S. and global cybersecurity efforts.

The good news is that many of the flawed aspects of the 2013 controls were improved pursuant to the outcomes of last year's Wassenaar plenary session, but the risks of further expansion of export controls to other cybersecurity technologies, or other technologies that could negatively impact either cybersecurity efforts or global data flows more broadly, remain. For instance, the European Union is currently in the process of redrafting its Dual-Use Export Regime, implicating many of these same issues.

These issues are not hypothetical – they are both very real and pervasive, insofar as they are not really limited to particular countries, regions or economies. I provide a "deep dive" on how these issues arise in several major markets below.

China. ITI members continue to be concerned with market access issues in China, especially barriers to entry portrayed as security justifications. China's discriminatory Cybersecurity Law (CSL) creates a legal framework that institutes multiple and overlapping security review regimes for foreign technology with limited transparency and significant ambiguity that can easily preference domestic industry. The security review regimes under the CSL and related measures compel companies to disclose sensitive information. The Law also contains "secure and controllable" requirements, which were raised in USTR's 2017 and 2016 National Trade Estimate (NTE) reports as a known issue with serious implications for domestic preferences. Moreover, the scope of the CSL is broad and several of its provisions remain ambiguous, conditions that will lead to problems with compliance.

Data localization measures have dramatically increased in China, jeopardizing not only the technology industry, but all other industries that depend on ICT platforms for global operations. Barriers that pre-dated the CSL already cost U.S. services billions of dollars as companies were pushed out of the market, with a vast majority of U.S. companies describing Chinese internet restrictions as either "somewhat negatively" or "negatively" impacting their capacity to do business there.[6] For instance, even though U.S. cloud service providers (CSPs) have stimulated innovation and application of cloud computing

---

[6] According to ITI member survey conducted in September 2016.

technologies around the world, China has imposed several onerous regulations on U.S. CSPs – effectively barring them from operating or competing fairly in China. Chinese laws and regulations on non-Chinese CSPs can force U.S. CSPs to transfer valuable intellectual property, surrender use of their brand names, and hand over operation and control of their businesses to Chinese companies in order to operate in China.

Embedded within the Cybersecurity Law and among numerous regulations and standards are requirements to store, process, or manage data locally within China and restrictions on flows of data in and out of China. The most prominent restrictions are found in the *Measures on Cross-Border Data Transfer* and the *Critical Information Infrastructure Protection Regulation*. The CSL creates additional barriers by mandating data localization for CII network owners and operators in China and restricting flows of data out of China.

These measures directly affect the ability of many industries beyond the tech sector to conduct normal business operations. This trend toward increased control over where and how data is transferred represents a destructive and misguided attempt to protect Chinese tech companies from foreign competition. Taken together, these measures pose great costs to U.S. firms in all sectors.

China also continues to flout international standards and norms, as demonstrated by an increase in laws and standards that include China-specific requirements. In April 2017, the State Encryption Management Bureau released the draft Encryption Law, which currently requires unique encryption of products and services within China that does not align with the Common Criteria.[7] The draft would also impose an intrusive licensing scheme covering the sale, use, and import or export of commercial cryptography that poses significant risks of disclosure for companies. Meanwhile, the draft Standardization Law causes concern among companies for its potential to create a burdensome standards regime. In establishing a framework for standards-making, the draft Standardization Law contains unclear definitions of standards types and their status as mandatory or voluntary. Numerous Chinese standards that are categorized as voluntary continue to be regarded by Chinese government agencies as mandatory or de facto mandatory, a problem that the law has not adequately addressed.

Beyond the negative impacts on U.S. companies in terms of access to the Chinese market itself, perhaps most worrisome is the potential of the CSL to emerge as the dominant approach to cyber policy in the region, or even globally.

India. India presents a unique case, insofar as the U.S. and India in 2016 successfully negotiated a bilateral agreement, the Framework for the U.S.-India Cyber Relationship, that seems to run counter to many of the problematic policies India continues to pursue.

In May 2017, India's Telecommunications Engineering Centre (TEC) proposed changes mandating certification and local testing for all telecom products regulated under India's Telegraph Rules. These changes are set to begin in October 2018 and include a wide range of technical requirements from electromagnetic compatibility (EMC) and safety to security testing and IPv6 interoperability, as well as environmental requirements, among others. TEC and the Department of Telecommunications (DoT) have not provided a rationale or details on the implementation this broad certification framework, nor have they notified it to the WTO Technical Barriers to Trade Committee for global stakeholder feedback.

---

[7] Common Criteria is the technical basis for the Common Criteria Recognition Arrangement (CCRA), an internationally-employed technical certification and mutual recognition agreement for secure IT products.

Many of these requirements will likely be redundant with existing international testing and certification of telecom products. Moreover, India has little capacity to or infrastructure to implement these changes. ITI and local industry are asking TEC/DoT to pare back the initial scope of the requirements and ITI is seeking clarification on many outstanding issues before TEC/DoT move ahead. ITI is also urging the authorities to follow global best practices and accept international test reports and certificates when applicable, and to allow for additional consultation with industry and an adequate transition time.

DoT also continues to pursue a mandate that telecom companies, operating networks within India and overseas, put in place necessary systems to ensure the networks within India's geographical borders comply with telecom security rules. In April 2013, DoT identified certain telecom products to be screened at an authorized test lab, of which some were singled out as "high risk items" to be checked from October 1, 2013. DoT notified industry that all imported telecom and ICT products (if internet connected) will have to be locally tested by DoT-accredited labs even if such devices have been screened by private labs within the Common Criteria Recognition Arrangement (CCRA) alliance. However, since notifying this requirement, DoT has delayed implementation every year since due to a lack of capacity for testing and unclear requirements for implementers. This measure, if ever implemented, would impose significant costs to U.S. companies exporting to India, and yearly last-minute delays in implementation have created significant uncertainty for companies exporting to India.

India maintains and is expanding local preferences for government procurement. Historically, the most prominent measure—*Preferential Market Access for Government Procurement (PMA-G)*—has steadily expanded from low level computing systems to high end servers and other technology products. This measure, implemented by MEITY and DoT, requires products to have certain levels of local content in order to qualify for procurement price preferences, effectively blocking many American companies from competing. However, in June 2017, the Department of Industrial Policy and Promotion released a new "Make in India" Order which gives a 20% price preference to all products with 50% Indian local content in government procurement. As a result, both MEITY and DoT are updating their PMA-G policies to reflect this order, expanding both the scope and effect of their policies. In addition, MEITY recently released a notification that will expand this program to cybersecurity products – a sector in which the U.S. has a significant competitive advantage. These requirements are extremely problematic for American tech companies that wish to do business in India, and the expansion on PMA to cybersecurity products is particularly problematic to the extent it necessarily impacts companies' intellectual property rights. When implemented, ITI member companies would be unable to compete fairly for government ICT contracts, which make up a large portion of the Indian ICT market.

In addition, the Telecommunications Regulatory Authority of India (TRAI) has published several consultation papers on a range of issues (cloud computing, machine to machine communications, data protection, and more). Though few concrete steps have yet been taken as a result of these consultations, many of them have explored potentially damaging policy options – most notably data localization and extending telecommunications regulations to OTT service providers. The outcomes of these consultations warrant attention from the USG as they could result in restricting the ability of U.S. companies to export their services to India in the future.

Russia. Russia has adopted several forced localization policies and laws. Federal Law 242-FZ, which requires data collected on Russian citizens to be stored in Russia, came into effect on September 1, 2015. This law affects the normal business operations of all industries in Russia by imposing inefficient operational rules, particularly the requirement in Article 18 to store personal data concerning Russian

citizens in data centers located in Russia. It appears that Roskomnadzor, the federal regulator responsible for implementation, has accepted mirroring of data—keeping copies of data within Russia rather than the more extensive requirements of processing it in-country—to be compliant with the law. However, the vague language in the law could allow for blocking cross-border data flows in the future, lending to an uncertain business environment in Russia. Furthermore, even mirroring of data can be very costly to businesses, particularly Small and Medium Size Enterprises (SME), increasing barriers to entry for the Russian market. In addition, the federal media regulator has been empowered to block local access to the websites of non-compliant companies. Given the law's expansive scope, foreign companies without a legal presence in Russia, which might pay only a cursory attention to the Russian market, can be labelled data protection violators and blocked. In late 2016, Russia began conducting audits and fining companies for violations. In one high profile case, this audit resulted in a U.S. internet company being blocked outright from doing business in Russia.

In January 2016, the Kremlin issued a 16-point plan for improving the competitiveness and security of the Russian ICT sector through import-substitution, increased surveillance capabilities, and increased education on issues related to cyber. The plan is focused on import substitution and has generally been talked about in the context of "internet sovereignty." Two new executive decrees associated with this plan call for ministries to create plans that prioritize Russian-produced software and equipment for government purchases, create additional obligations for how the personal information of Russian citizens is processed, regulate the encryption of data, reorganize federal cyber-threat monitoring, and establish a Center of Import Substitution for Information and Communication Technologies. In October 2016, a bill was introduced in the Duma that would further require government entities to provide preferences even to Russian developed software that is based on foreign-developed middleware. Further implementation and follow-up decrees have been opaque and seemingly poorly coordinated, so there is little information on how the plan has progressed.

Federal Law No. 149-FZ *"On Information, Information Technologies and the Protection of Information,"* as amended in 2014, has two particularly troubling elements. First, Article 10.1 *"The Duties of an Organizer of Dissemination of Information on the Internet,"* requires "organizers of the distribution of information on the internet" to retain all metadata within Russia for six months and provide access to that data to security agencies. This applies to an incredibly wide range of companies that facilitate the receipt, transmission, delivery, and/or processing of electronic messages—including any email and internet-based messaging services. Second, Article 10.2, the "Blogger's Law," requires bloggers with more than 3,000 daily users to register with Roskomnadzor and places restrictions on what they can and cannot post to their websites. This law not only has significant free speech and human right implications, but it also creates costly barriers for U.S. companies who wish to do business in Russia.

Lastly, on July 7th, 2016 President Putin signed a package laws (374-FZ and 375-FZ) that amended Russian Federal Laws 126-FZ and 149-FZ—known as the *"Yarovaya Amendments."* These amendments require "organizers of information distribution on the internet" to store the content of communications that they enable within Russia for six months. In addition, telecommunications companies must store metadata of all communications within Russia for three years, whereas "organizers," referring to internet providers, must store metadata for one year. If any of this data in encrypted, then companies must also provide encryption keys to the implementing agency, the Federal Security Service (FSB). These requirements will be incredibly costly for companies operating in Russia, so much so that domestic telecommunications companies have been in vocal opposition to the law, a rare event in the country.

European Union. There are also a range of policy and regulatory proposals related to security and privacy in the EU that potentially jeopardize data flows.

E-Privacy Regulation. The European Commission unveiled its draft proposal for an ePrivacy Regulation (ePR) last year. The ePR is a priority issue for ITI and our members for several reasons, including the broad material, definitional and territorial scope of the proposed regulation's reach, prescriptiveness of its provisions, size of contemplated penalties/fines, and inefficiencies and confusion caused by overlap and conflict with the GDPR. While it is hard to single out just a few concerning provisions, perhaps most troubling of all is simply the vast scope of electronic communication services (ECS) data the draft proposes to regulate – the "Regulation applies to any exchange of information using electronic communication services and public communications networks, including content and metadata," and expressly applies not only to OTTs but communications among IoT devices, including machine-to-machine communications, and thus directly impacting three of the leading edge data-driven innovations. As for the penalties, fines for violations of the ePR can range as high as the greater of €20M, or 4% of worldwide revenue. ITI has also pointed out potentially problematic unintended consequences of the ePR on cybersecurity, particularly on the ability of companies to retain third party cybersecurity providers to defend their networks due to rigid consent and other requirements. ITI will continue to advocate for changes to ePR to minimize the impacts on important emerging technology priority areas such as artificial intelligence, OTTs and IoT.

Safe Harbor Invalidation and Privacy Shield. Most are aware the transatlantic trade relationship was legitimately placed in serious jeopardy back in 2015, when the invalidation of the Safe Harbor agreement by the Court of Justice of the European Union (CJEU) ruling in *Maximillian Schrems v. Data Protection Commissioner* (Case C-362/14) ("*Schrems*") cast uncertainty on the ability of companies to transfer data from the EU to the U.S. While the U.S.-EU Privacy Shield arrangement, which took effect on August 1, 2016, and was recently reaffirmed by the European Commission following the first joint annual review of the agreement, represents a strong commitment by both the U.S. and EU to enable transfers of data across the Atlantic and safeguard consumer privacy, threats to transatlantic data flows remain due primarily to two factors: 1) the pending judicial review at the European Court of Justice of standard contractual clauses, which give U.S. companies an alternative option to ensure that they can transfer data from the EU to the U.S., and 2) challenges in other EU courts to the Privacy Shield itself.

EU Cybersecurity Measures. The Network and Information Security Directive (NIS Directive), the first EU-wide cybersecurity legislation, must be transposed into member state law by May 2018, and the threat of siloed approaches (across the member states) to implementation on key issues, such as the scope of NIS application to technology companies and the potential of asymmetric security incident notification requirements (including rationalizing them vis-a-vis the GDPR's data breach notification requirements), remains. While Germany's legislation implementing NIS is already largely in place, and the UK (who is implementing NIS despite its impending departure from the EU due to Brexit) released their draft legislation to transpose the Directive late last year, several other member states have yet to release legislation to transpose or implement NIS at all, making it hard to fully gauge the risks of regulatory fragmentation. In the latter part of last year, the European Commission also released a comprehensive "cybersecurity package" including a revision and update of the 2011 Cybersecurity Strategy and Proposal for a Regulation on ENISA (the EU Agency for Network and Information Security), the "EU Cybersecurity Agency," and on information and communication technology cybersecurity certification

(the "Cybersecurity Act").[8] Key issues of concern with the proposals include the overbroad and potentially far-reaching scope of the cybersecurity certification scheme, the potential for it to be linked to EU rather than international standards, and the current lack of ENISA resources to support its vastly expanded mandate.

Recent U.S. Cyber Policy Activity in the Global Context

On balance, recent cyber policy activity in the U.S. acknowledges both the importance of global data flows and avoids many of the policy pitfalls identified above. *The Cyber Diplomacy Act of 2017* (CDA) helpfully recounts many of the noteworthy cyber policy initiatives advanced or supported by the U.S. over the past several years that are not only supportive of data flows, but necessarily depend on prioritizing and resourcing international approaches to address our shared cyber challenges, including:

- 2011 U.S. International Strategy for Cyberspace
- 2016 International Cyberspace Policy Strategy
- 2016 Commission on Enhancing National Cybersecurity
- Multilateral declarations at the G-7 and G-20
- May 2017 Executive Order on Cybersecurity (EO 13800)

To that list, I would add the Framework for Improving Critical Infrastructure Cybersecurity (the "**Cybersecurity Framework**"), a voluntary, risk management framework grounded in international standards and best practices that was co-developed by NIST and other USG stakeholders in partnership with industry, and the *Cybersecurity Act of 2015*,[9] bipartisan **information sharing legislation** expressly designed to increase the flow of information for cybersecurity purposes. Additionally, some of the initial outputs spurred by the **EO 13800**, including the **botnet report**,[10] similarly acknowledge the importance of the international dimension of cyber policy.

All these policies, spanning both the Obama and Trump Administrations, implicate ecosystem-wide, global cyber challenges calling for global solutions advanced via international and public-private partnerships and collaboration.

The Cyber Diplomacy Act of 2017. The CDA is a welcome and complementary contribution to this recent body of U.S. cyber policymaking that appears to strike the right chord on multiple fronts. Of particular note are the following elements of the bill:

Taking a Global Approach That Promotes Data Flows, Innovation, Openness and Economic Prosperity. The CDA's expression of the overarching policy objectives it is trying to achieve fairly encapsulates the types of cyber policy approaches that help promote data flows, innovation and economic prosperity, and that ITI routinely promotes: *"Congress declares that it is the policy of the United States to work internationally with allies and other partners to promote an open, interoperable, reliable, unfettered and*

---

[8] See Proposal for a Regulation on ENISA, the "EU Cybersecurity Agency", and repealing Regulation (EU) 526/2013, and on Information and Communication Technology cybersecurity certification ("Cybersecurity Act").

[9] Consolidated Appropriations Act, 2016, H.R. 2029, 114th Cong., Division N (2015).

[10] See NTIA's Draft "Report to the President on Enhancing the Resilience of the internet and Communications Ecosystem Against Botnets and Other Automated, Distributed Threats" at: https://www.ntia.doc.gov/files/ntia/publications/eo_13800_botnet_report_for_public_comment.pdf

secure internet governed by the multistakeholder model which promotes human rights, democracy, and rule of law, including freedom of expression, innovation, communication, and economic prosperity, while protecting privacy and guarding against deception, fraud and theft." (Sec. 3(a))

Securing and implementing commitments based on cyber policy norms. The CDA prioritizes several commitments to pursue to advance cyber policy norms that would help mitigate the problematic global policies detailed earlier in my testimony, including:

- Furthering cross border data flows by prohibiting localization
- Incentivizing security by design
- Shielding critical infrastructure entities and CERTS from state-sponsored attacks
- Avoiding state-sponsored IP theft to provide commercial advantages to the private sector

Actionable and accountable agreements. The CDA also smartly seeks to establish guardrails designed to make those agreements both actionable and accountable. The CDA compiles a list of existing **bilateral cyber agreements** with nine countries. Over the past several years The Department of State and other key USG stakeholders such as the Departments of Homeland Security (DHS) and Commerce have done an admirable job of forging a series of cyber bilateral agreements consistent with the governing principles articulated above. As the CDA points out, however, there is a need to follow through by making "evidence-based assessments" regarding the functioning of those agreements, to make sure our counterparties are fulfilling their commitments and other obligations. **Multilateral agreements** are also a clear part of the solution to furthering international progress on cybersecurity and other cyber policy issues, and the bill acknowledges important foundational work that has already been done at the G7 and G20. This is one area, perhaps, where the CDA could more specifically call out the need for actionable and accountable follow through, as it does explicitly in the context of bilateral agreements.

Prioritizing and Allocating Department of State Resources. Realizing the international cyber policy objectives expressed in the bill will require adequately prioritizing and allocating sufficient resources, including regarding the Cyber Coordinator role at the State Department.

The CDA proposes the Department of State cyber coordinator should be a Senate-confirmed position at the rank of ambassador. This makes good sense for several reasons. First, the rank and title of the position sends an important message to other countries regarding the importance the USG places on the cyber issues falling within the coordinator's purview. Second, the practical reality is whoever resides in this position will often have to negotiate with counterparts at other countries holding a similar rank – these counterparts need to know they are dealing with a peer with proportionate decision-making authority. Finally, staffing the position at a senior level can aid in interagency discussions with peer decisionmakers at DHS, Commerce and other USG stakeholders, and can help provide greater continuity through subsequent administrations and personnel changes.

The scope and scale of cyber issues facing the U.S. and the Department of State is growing - we urge that the cyber coordinator's office be adequately resourced to handle this mandate. As the next wave of emerging technologies and digital innovations continue to take hold, cyber issues will only continue to grow in breadth and prominence as policy, economic and security issues for the United States, and the Department of State's lead cyber official and office should be adequately resourced to handle them.

Recommendations

My testimony thus far should make clear there are landmines all over the global cyber policy landscape. While it's instructive to understand where they are, and the stated and unstated motivations underlying them, what's more important for the USG is defining and resourcing a collaborative, proactive strategy, in partnership with the private sector, to drive forward the admirable policy objectives expressed in the CDL. Ultimately, helping that global, open, innovation-friendly approach gain traction will be the best way to influence those countries at earlier stages of cyber policy development in a direction that supports the policy objectives shared by the USG and industry – not simply because we support them, but because those are the policies that will ultimately help developing countries fulfill their internet-fueled economic and digital aspirations.

Below are concrete recommendations for USG actions internationally that can help improve global data flows, security, and the other international cyber objectives expressed in the CDA.

Continue to Prioritize and Resource International Cybersecurity Standardization. To counter the trend of various countries increasingly advocating for their own local security standards, testing protocols, certifications, etc., it seems obvious the U.S. needs a proactive and adequately resourced national strategy involving both industry and government working together to develop and further international cybersecurity standards, consistent with the policy expressed in the CDA. The U.S. has already made some progress in this area, including the Interagency Report on Strategic U.S. Government Engagement in International Standardization to Achieve U.S. Objectives for Cybersecurity (the "International Standardization Strategy") published by NIST in 2016. We recommend that the current administration prioritize furthering this strategy to improve the U.S. government's participation in the development and use of international standards for cybersecurity, as well as IoT, AI and other emerging standards areas. Doing so will require a unity of effort with industry, as well as adequate resources and political support.

Further the Cybersecurity Framework Approach Globally. The Cybersecurity Framework approach represents the most prominent counterweight to many of the data-restrictive policy approaches recounted above and that are growing in prominence globally. The Framework leverages public-private partnerships, is grounded in sound risk management principles, and helps foster innovation due to its flexibility and basis in global standards. The Framework has also consistently been lauded for providing a common language to better help organizations comprehend, communicate and manage cybersecurity risks – it can serve as a common language for global policymakers as well. International Cybersecurity Framework alignment is essential to its longevity, and foundational to driving such alignment involves the global Framework promotion efforts of both industry and government. Promoting the Framework in its current form will help the U.S. to sustain its leadership on cybersecurity around the world, and this will in turn help to further enhance the Framework's use within the United States. To facilitate further global adoption, USG stakeholders should promote the Framework approach with their global counterparts. For example, the Department of State should reference the Framework in its global cybersecurity capacity-building efforts. Likewise, the White House should highlight the Framework in its strategic cybersecurity partnerships. ITI has also urged NIST to explore, with industry stakeholders, the opportunity for submitting relevant parts of the Framework as an international standard. The latest draft of the Roadmap to Framework Version 1.1 indicates NIST has actively engaged with the ISO and IEC to map existing international standards to the Framework, work that has led to the anticipated publication of an ISO/IEC Technical Report.

Leverage Multilateral Fora to Drive Cyber Policy Solutions. Multilateral agreements are also a clear part of the solution to furthering global progress on cybersecurity and other cyber policy issues, and the CDA references important foundational work that has already been done at the G7 and G20. While not all multilateral fora hold equal promise, ultimately pursuing multilateral solutions in parallel with bilateral ones can be an important force multiplier to drive policy solutions across the global digital economy. For example, good progress has been made at the Asia-Pacific Economic Cooperation (APEC) forum to further the Cross-Border Privacy Rules (CBPRs) framework. The APEC CBPRs are flexible enough to be adopted on a broad scale and are gaining traction across a diverse set of economies in the APEC region, providing a mechanism to move data safely between organizations while providing a bridge to address variations in laws or regulatory fragmentation amongst the participating economies. The United States, Mexico, Canada, Japan, South Korea, Singapore, the Philippines and Australia are already participating or have committed to participate in the CBPRs, and other APEC economies have signaled their interest in joining. The CBPRs offer a scalable system that holds the potential to be less burdensome to economies and companies than navigating other more restrictive, burdensome, resource-intensive, data transfer mechanisms.

Conclusion

Members of the committee, ITI and our member companies are pleased you are examining the role and importance of cyber diplomacy in a world of evolving and increasingly sophisticated threats. Unfortunately, government policymakers globally are increasingly responding to the expanding sophistication and capabilities of cyber adversaries and more frequent and severe cyber incidents by proposing cyber laws and policies that can create trade barriers for U.S. companies and threaten to impede cross-border data flows. If left unchecked, this activity threatens to undermine both the trust and interoperability undergirding the global digital ecosystem.

Historically, the U.S. has maintained a leadership position in cyberspace – from the companies who have led the way in building the global digital economy and internet-based services that have fueled its growth, to visionary cyber policy developments such as the Cybersecurity Framework, to pioneering bilateral cyber agreements negotiated with allied and competitor nations alike. If the USG aspires to maintain its leadership position going forward, it must not only work collectively – both domestically and on the global stage, bilaterally and multilaterally, via public-private collaboration and across sectors – but it must lead.

ITI stands ready to provide you any additional input and assistance in our collaborative efforts to develop balanced policy approaches that help all of us to collectively advance cyber policies that promote global data flows, innovation, security, economic prosperity, and the other laudable objectives expressed in the *Cyber Diplomacy Act*.

I thank the Chairman, Ranking Member, and Members of the Committee for inviting me to testify today and for their interest in and examination of this important issue. I look forward to your questions.

Thank you.

Chairman ROYCE. Thank you, Mr. Miller.
Dr. Sulmeyer.

STATEMENT OF MICHAEL SULMEYER, PH.D., DIRECTOR, CYBER SECURITY PROJECT, BELFER CENTER FOR SCIENCE AND INTERNATIONAL AFFAIRS, JOHN F. KENNEDY SCHOOL OF GOVERNMENT, HARVARD UNIVERSITY (FORMER DIRECTOR FOR PLANS AND OPERATIONS FOR CYBER POLICY, OFFICE OF THE SECRETARY OF DEFENSE, U.S. DEPARTMENT OF DEFENSE)

Mr. SULMEYER. Chairman Royce, Ranking Member Engel, and distinguished members of the Foreign Affairs Committee, it is an honor to be with you today to discuss U.S. cyber diplomacy. Thank you for bipartisan approach to cybersecurity. I will keep my remarks brief. Three topics to focus on: The first, the international environment for cyber diplomacy; the second, the challenges of deterrence; and third, our elections.

First, we need diplomacy in cyberspace now more than ever. Our adversaries continue to refine their capabilities to conduct a range of cyber operations against us. We have developed offensive cyber capabilities and hardened our defenses, yet hackers keep hacking our systems.

Under Chris Painter's leadership, the State Department pursued international efforts to promote norms of responsible State behavior. This effort gained momentum, especially during the latter years of the Obama administration, as did efforts to negotiate bilateral arrangements, like the U.S.-China agreement. The current administration has, thus far, for pursued more bilateral arrangements, like the one it announced with Israel last summer. Yet, my impression is that most state behavior, not state rhetoric, reflects a perception in international capitals that the benefits of unrestrained hacking outweigh the costs.

For the time being, the United States will likely need to focus on discrete, bilateral arrangements, while protecting U.S. interests and existing international institutions. Having a dedicated office at the State Department is crucial to pursuing both objectives. But for diplomacy to be successful, the United States needs to empower its diplomats with as much leverage as possible. One approach to creating more leverage is to improve our ability to deter adversaries from hacking us. In an ideal world, it would be a tremendous help if these threats could be deterred by one common approach. But the reality is far more complicated. Not all hacks are the same, so we should not expect a one-size-fits-all model of deterrence to be successful.

Attacks against critical infrastructure certainly warrant the threat of significant cost imposition. In some situations, however, deterrence in the criminal law context, which aims to minimize but not necessarily eliminate the incidence of the crime, seems more applicable, especially to run-of-the-mill hacking, than an analogy to nuclear weapons. I would not want to bet the cybersecurity of the United States on a policy of deterrence if I did not have to. Sometimes, like the prospect of defending against thousands of nuclear-tipped missiles, deterrence is the least bad option. But this is not the case in cyberspace. We have other options, and we should employ them alongside deterrence. But we must be realistic about just how much we can expect from deterrence.

So what does this mean when it comes to dealing with Russia, which launched a cyber-enabled influence campaign against us in 2016? Deterring a repeat of this conduct must be a priority for the entire U.S. Government, and indeed for all nations whose elections are susceptible to Russian interference. The need to impose cost is clear. But the challenge is to impose it in ways that matter to the Russian regime, not in ways that are projections of what would matter to the United States.

However, we cannot rely on deterrence alone. We need to ensure that the United States has capabilities on the shelf to prevent and preempt this kind of behavior ahead of the midterms, and we must make ourselves harder to hack through improving our defenses and becoming more resilient.

I am proud to be part of a team at the Belfer Center that is releasing a new report this morning, a playbook for State and local officials to improve the cybersecurity of the systems they administer. It represents the culmination of months of fieldwork by the research team including some exceptionally talented students which developed recommendations to prepare for the upcoming elections. We also have a playbook to help campaigns protect themselves from hackers. Both reports can be helpful for our allies as well who face similar threats. Both are available on our Web site.

There is every indication that foreign governments will try to sow confusion ahead of and during the next election. This should be of concern to every American, regardless of party. Improving the cybersecurity of campaigns as well as at the State and local level, both at home and abroad, needs to be a core element of a broader strategy to push back against our adversaries who seek to undermine the confidence we have in the integrity of our elections.

Let me conclude my opening remarks by reiterating my appreciation for this committee's bipartisan approach. I look forward to taking your questions.

[The prepared statement of Mr. Sulmeyer follows:]

Testimony of Michael Sulmeyer
Director of the Cyber Security Project
Belfer Center for Science and International Affairs
Harvard Kennedy School
House Foreign Affairs Committee
U.S. Cyber Diplomacy in an Era of Growing Threats
February 6, 2018

Chairman Royce, Ranking Member Engel, and distinguished members of the U.S. House of Representatives Foreign Affairs Committee, it is an honor to be with you today to discuss U.S. cyber diplomacy. I begin by noting my appreciation for the committee's bipartisan approach to cybersecurity. I note the bipartisan support for the Ukraine Cybersecurity Cooperation Act of 2017 and the Cyber Diplomacy Act of 2017, among others. As cybersecurity has become an increasingly important aspect of U.S. foreign policy, bipartisan support for keeping our country safe and protecting America's interests is essential.

I will keep my prepared remarks brief, focusing on three topics:
- The current international environment for cyber diplomacy,
- The challenges of deterring malicious cyber activity, and
- Cybersecurity and information operations in the context of our elections.

I. The current international environment for cyber diplomacy

To put it bluntly, we need diplomacy in cyberspace now more than ever. Our competitors and adversaries continue to refine their capabilities to conduct a range of cyber operations, from criminal extortion and gaining unauthorized access to networks of U.S. companies, to attempting to meddle with our elections and compromise our critical infrastructure. Despite our significant investments to develop offensive cyber capabilities and to harden defenses across the country, hackers keep hacking our systems, as well as those of our allies and partners.

Under Chris Painter's leadership, the State Department pursued international efforts to promote norms of responsible state behavior in cyberspace. This effort gained momentum during the latter years of the last administration, as did efforts to negotiate bilateral arrangements, like the U.S.-China agreement on cyber-enabled espionage for private gain against U.S. companies. The current administration has thus far pursued bilateral arrangements, like the one it announced with Israel last summer.

There are starkly divergent views among nations about the role of the Internet in society. Diplomacy and engagement is critical to ensuring the open, multi-stakeholder Internet prevails. The alternative is a closed system, governed by nations that police the content of what their own citizens express online. This is the Internet of Russia and China, not America.

Yet I do not believe there is a sufficient international appetite for a grand deal or treaty to restrain unwanted activity in cyberspace. My impression is that most state behavior—not state rhetoric—reflects a perception in international capitals that the benefits of unrestrained hacking outweigh the costs. For the time being, the United States will likely need to focus on discrete, bilateral arrangements while protecting U.S. interests in existing international institutions. Having a dedicated office at the State Department is crucial to pursuing both objectives. I also hope that such an office would take an active role in increasing the technical knowledge and training for the diplomats of today and tomorrow.

II. The challenges of deterring malicious cyber activity

For diplomacy to be successful, the United States needs to empower its diplomats with as much leverage as possible. One oft-discussed approach to creating more leverage and increasing U.S. relative power in cyberspace is to improve our ability to deter adversaries from hacking us. In an ideal world, it would be a tremendous help if these threats could be deterred by one common approach. However, the reality is far more complicated.

Not all hacks are the same, so we should not expect a one-size-fits-all model of deterrence to be successful. Attacks against critical infrastructure certainly warrant the threat of significant cost imposition, as the Obama and Trump Administrations have articulated. In some situations, deterrence in the criminal law context—which aims to minimize but not necessarily eliminate the incidence of crimes—seems more applicable to run of the mill malicious hacking, even by foreign governments, than an analogy to nuclear weapons.

I would not want to bet the cybersecurity of the United States on a policy of deterrence if I did not have to. Sometimes, like the prospect of defending against thousands of nuclear-tipped missiles, deterrence is the least bad option. That is not the case in cybersecurity. We have other options and we should employ them alongside deterrence. Pursuing strategies to prevent and preempt adversaries from being able to conduct serious cyber attacks against the United States is critical. Also, there remains so much to do to improve our defenses and our resilience in the face of incoming attacks. Success there, should, over time, bolster U.S. security and leverage for broader diplomatic efforts. However, we must be realistic about just how much we can expect from deterrence, and who we want to deter from doing what.

III. Cybersecurity and information operations in the context of our elections.

What does this mean when it comes to dealing with Russia, which launched a cyber-enabled influence campaign against us in 2016? Deterring a repeat of this conduct must be a priority for the entire U.S. government, and indeed for all nations whose elections are susceptible to Russian interference. The need to impose cost is clear, but the challenge is to impose it in ways that matter to the Russian regime—not in ways that are projections of what would matter to the United States. However, we cannot rely on deterrence alone: we need to ensure the United States has capabilities on the shelf to prevent and preempt this kind of behavior ahead of the midterms, and we must make ourselves harder to hack through improving our defenses and becoming more resilient.

I am proud to be part of a team at the Belfer Center that is releasing a new report this morning: a playbook for state and local officials with steps they can take to improve the cybersecurity of the systems they administer. It represents the culmination of months of fieldwork by the research team, including several exceptionally talented students, which developed 10 recommendations that state and local officials can consider as they prepare for the upcoming elections:

- Create a proactive security culture,
- Treat elections as an interconnected system,
- Have a paper vote record,
- Use audits to show transparency and maintain trust in the elections process,
- Implement strong passwords and two-factor authentication,
- Control and actively manage access,
- Prioritize and isolate sensitive data and systems,
- Monitor, log, and backup data,
- Require vendors to make security a priority, and
- Build public trust and prepare for information operations.

These recommendations complement our last playbook, which contained recommendations for political campaigns to improve their cybersecurity. Both reports can be downloaded from our website, belfercenter.org.

Implementing these recommendations will make our elections harder to hack. Also, proposals from both playbooks can be used by our allies and partners to bolster their defenses as well. Improving the cybersecurity of campaigns as well as at the state and local level, both at home and abroad, needs to be a core element of a broader strategy to push back against our competitors and adversaries who seek to undermine the confidence we have in the integrity of our elections.

There is every indication that foreign governments will try to sow confusion and chaos ahead of and during the next election. This should be of concern to every American, regardless of party affiliation. While I do not expect that the political divisions in Washington will be resolved by November, I hope there is growing agreement that we should not leave our elections vulnerable to foreign interference again.

Let me conclude my opening remarks by reiterating my appreciation for this committee's bipartisan approach to cybersecurity. I look forward to taking your questions.

###

Chairman ROYCE. Thank you.

Thank you. Let me just begin by saying what we in the House have advocated here in the legislation that we passed that I authored, along with Mr. Engel, has been to call for a Cyber Diplomacy Act, I think, is unique. We are not simply asking the Department to maintain the cyber coordinator. What we are asking for here is the creation of a cyber bureau headed by the Senate-confirmed Assistant Secretary, and the Bureau and its leaders, then, are empowered, as they must be, are empowered to deal with a full range of cyber issues, including security, including economy, including human rights. So that is the approach the House is taking, and the Senate has been receptive to that idea.

So let me go with my question here, Mr. Painter, if I could, or Mr. Miller.

So China has emerged as a very aggressive power in cyberspace. And in addition to China's articulation of this idea of cyber sovereignty, Beijing is now aggressively pushing U.S. companies to turn over its technological know-how as the cost of assessing China's enormous market. Obviously, it is in both our national security and economic interest to respond to this technology grab there, and one proposal is to strengthen CFIUS, the Committee on Foreign Investment in the United States. This committee is looking at a complementary approach of strengthening our export controls in tandem.

So, Mr. Miller, if I could start with you. How does the technology industry see this threat, since they have got the most to lose here, and how can Congress best respond?

Mr. MILLER. Thank you for your question, Chairman Royce.

Well, in terms of the threat, the technology industry has been consistent in advocating against any policies globally that would require companies to turn over or provide access to source code to governments anywhere. So, it is certainly very concerning indeed.

You referenced the efforts that are underway to update, modernize the CFIUS process. In terms of the underlying national security concerns that are articulated in that bill with respect to the transfers of technologies that are critical to U.S. national security interests, you know, absolutely, the tech sector agrees that that is a serious concern. As you pointed out, it is highlighted in some of these approaches. You know, the question is whether the bill is narrowly tailored to address that goal, or whether it sweeps in all kinds of ordinary business transactions that do not involve the transfer of critical technology, or whether it involves—it might sweep in transactions that are already adequately covered or should be adequately covered by the export control regime.

From our perspective, what we are working to ensure is an approach that addresses the underlying national security concerns in a targeted fashion without negatively impacting those daily business transactions or creating kind of a parallel duplicative export control regime. From our perspective, ultimately export controls and CFIUS should work in a complementary, not a duplicative fashion. And we believe there is a way to both update and optimize the current export control system to cover emerging technologies, for instance, and also to update CFIUS in a targeted way that makes sense and helps supplement that.

Chairman ROYCE. Well, let me ask Mr. Painter, also, his views on this.

Mr. PAINTER. Yeah. I think it is clear that China has become much more aggressive on the world stage. Among other things, one of the counterparts I had that was created after our office was created was China. China and Russia created counterparts. And they have their own international strategy they put out about a year ago which champions this idea of absolute sovereignty. And they also, as you noted, had been passing laws in the guise of cybersecurity that are often more about market protection. It is a difficult issue because I think one of the things that we have seen is they become active in working diplomatically with other countries and trying to, quite frankly, build alliances with a developing world and others to really further their own view of cyberspace.

On the company side, we have made some progress. As you know, the agreement with China not to steal intellectual property by cyber means, that was a landmark agreement. It took a while to get us there and a lot of pressure to get us there. That was very helpful.

Chairman ROYCE. How about on the enforcement side of that?

Mr. PAINTER. Well, I—no. I think what we said then, and we—and this is still the policy as far as I know now, is all tools are on the table. We didn't take anything off the table to get that agreement. And sanctions and other tools are there, and we have to think of other tools still.

I do worry that, you know, when I see U.S. companies faced with this, and I have dealt with a number of them, they are often unwilling individually to express these issues because they are concerned about the market issues in China. Trade associations, ITI and others, I think, have been very good interlocutors about this. But that is one of the issues.

The other thing I worry about is even if you look at CFIUS and other types of legislation, which are not exactly tailored to this problem, there are things that China is doing in terms of joint ventures and other things that really don't fall within that rubric. So how do you really address this problem in a broader sense? And I think it takes looking at a lot of different tools including——

Chairman ROYCE. And that is why we will be consultation with you on the export controls and on the——

Let's go to Dr. Sulmeyer.

Do you have any insights that you could share with us on this?

Mr. SULMEYER. On this particular topic, I agree with my colleagues, but would emphasize the need to strengthen CFIUS. I think that is a critical priority.

Chairman ROYCE. Very good.

We go to Mr. Engel.

Mr. ENGEL. Thank you, Mr. Chairman.

First, quickly, I would like to start by asking all of our witnesses just a quick yes or no to set the record straight. We can start with Mr. Painter.

Do any of you have any reason to doubt the intelligence community's assessment that Russia interfered to influence our 2016 election?

Mr. PAINTER. None whatsoever.

Mr. MILLER. No.

Mr. SULMEYER. Nope.

Mr. ENGEL. Thank you.

Dr. Sulmeyer, the intelligence community reported that the Kremlin interfered to aid Donald Trump and damage Hillary Clinton's candidacy. The Trump administration's CIA Director said that the Russians have been doing this in other countries for years, and will do so again during our next election.

What is Russia's overall goal with this interference? What should the United States do that it is not doing to become more resilient and prepare itself for another round of Putin's election interference?

Mr. SULMEYER. Thank you. It is an important question, and it is a good baseline way to express first that these Russian activities form a broader part of a strategy that are not limited to cyberspace. They are operating in areas below what we would think of as war, but it is certainly not peace. And they are very active and have no shame in what they are willing to do and the tactics they are willing to employ in the so-called gray zones.

I think you can discern sometimes three different motives at times: One is very straightforward traditional espionage collection in ways to help military and intelligence goals. We have seen that against the United States in many different situations against government networks; two, the spread of, and sometimes, also, manufacture of disinformation. Here the objective being the creation of chaos and confusion that undermines their opponent's ability to actually discern the truth. It is not just hacking. It is not just a cyber question. It is the knowing introduction of false and fake information at the right times, at the right place, on the right topics, to make it so that it becomes much more difficult to get to the bottom of what is going on. The example you can easily point to is the shoot-down of the aircraft over Ukraine, and the disinformation put out there.

The third topic I will just hit briefly is the increasing desire on the part of the Russians to hold targets at risk. And this is about being able to affect and manipulate critical infrastructure targets when tensions get hot. And the example here would be taking out power in the Ukraine for a little while a couple years ago. We want to make sure that does not happen here, not at all.

Mr. ENGEL. Thank you.

Mr. Painter, I was disappointed when I heard that the administration downgraded the State Department cyber diplomacy office. Hopefully, the Cyber Diplomacy Act will elevate this office again. In the meantime, what do you think downgrading this office will mean for American leadership on cybersecurity and other critical issues?

Mr. PAINTER. So I very much hope that the trend reverses. I think we had built up a lot of momentum, and especially, we are in the midst of it, an Executive order on cyber dealing with diplomacy and other issues, and we had established a leadership position in the world, I think even if it was for a temporary period, stepping—or seeming to stepping back from the world stage really empowers our adversaries to try to exploit that and work to advance their agenda, and really gives our allies and partners a reason to question whether the U.S. is going to continue to lead and continue to prioritize these issues.

So I think that that was just not the right approach. I very much hope that between the act and other activities that we can elevate this again at the State Department. I think it is a key 21st century issue, and I hope that happens.

And if there is time, Congressman, I also would like to address the question that you just asked Mr. Sulmeyer, too, in terms of some of the things we can being doing. I agree we have not done enough to deter this activity. This will, in fact, happen again, as was stated by the Director of National Intelligence in both administrations, including Mike Pompeo recently. There is a number of things I think we can do actively, including having a clear declarative statement that this is something that we will not countenance. There will be consequences for this activity coming from the administration.

I think you could set up, and this is not my ideas, but talking to a lot of people in the community, including a lot of former government people and present ones, but we could set up a task force that will really deal with protecting our elections, knowing this is going to happen in 2018 and beyond that would involve dealing with social media and others, a real interagency task force that would be focused on this issue. I think we can enhance our deterrence tools. I think we do a bad job in deterrence, as I said before, across the board.

And then finally, I think there is a number of pieces of legislation, both in the Senate and the House side, that can give us greater tools to protect election systems. And there is a lot more that can be done there.

Mr. ENGEL. Mr. Painter, I want to ask you one final question.

As I mentioned in my statement, the President has refused, in my opinion, to hold Russia accountable for election interference. He has refused to impose sanctions, which clearly was in the legislation that we passed with over 400 votes on the House floor. So he has refused to impose sanctions or intensify efforts to prevent Putin from trying to undermine our next election.

Let me ask you this: What do you think the President should do in response to this last attack on our democracy and what message does our lack of action send?

Mr. PAINTER. I outlined some of this just now, but I would say that in deterrence, the classic parts of deterrence, other than the deterrence by denial, is that you have a credible response and you have a timely response. And consequences are important.

When I was a prosecutor, if we didn't prosecute people, they would be running around doing crimes every day, right? So you need to have consequences for bad actors, both to deter them and as a consequence of their actions. And if we don't take any action, that, itself, sets a norm of inaction. That makes the activity they are doing seem acceptable. And they will do it again. And I think it is very likely they will.

So given all that, I think we need to really use all the tools in our tool kit, including sanctions, to continue to send a clear message this is unacceptable. This was a very, very big deal. This is trying to undermine our democracy. Whatever side of the political spectrum you are on, this is a huge deal in the U.S. and around the world, and we have got to do everything we can to try to thwart it. And I think if you don't do actions and—to be sure, you can think of how you are strategically going to approach it. But if you don't do actions, that sends a clear message, Hey, this is okay. Or at least, Hey, this is a costless enterprise.

Mr. ENGEL. Thank you. I couldn't agree with you more.

Thank you.

Chairman ROYCE. Mr. Dana Rohrabacher.

Mr. ROHRABACHER. Thank you very much, Mr. Chairman, and thank you for providing leadership in this area, making sure we have a hearing and to a very important issue.

It is easy to see that we live in a different world than I grew up in. There was no Internet, and when people wanted to sabotage someone else's campaign, they didn't have to go onto the Internet or use cyber warfare in order to do it. But now we know that we have this vehicle. We are dependent on the Internet to do business. And when we talk about cyberattacks, we are talking about sometimes sabotaging someone, a system, so they can't work, or we are talking about the theft of information. And I don't know, frankly, these things were done beforehand, but now we have a new threat, a new challenge, because we have a new technology vehicle.

Mr. Miller, you just, in passing, noted that India and China and other countries beside Russia are engaged in this type of activity.

Mr. MILLER. Sure. Thank you for the question Representative Rohrabacher.

There are actually—if you look at some of the problematic policy provisions that I mentioned at the outset broadly, forced localization types of policies and requiring companies to store their data in-country, or you look at some of the potential requests for security testing to be conducted by government auditors, those types of proposals do exist in India specifically.

Mr. ROHRABACHER. So we have a lot of hacking going on——

Mr. MILLER. Right.

Mr. ROHRABACHER [continuing]. In this arena, not just in Russia, but throughout the world.

By the way, does our Government engage in using the Internet to place false stories about people we consider our adversaries?

Mr. MILLER. I really have no personal knowledge of what the government is doing in that regard.

Mr. ROHRABACHER. What about you? Does the United States do this?

Mr. SULMEYER. I have no direct knowledge of that.

Mr. ROHRABACHER. Oh, so we don't know. We know all about the Russians doing it, but we don't know if our own Government does the same thing?

I would suggest that maybe our Government does the same thing quite often, and having direct knowledge of several instances of that.

Now, with that said, let me just ask this——

Mr. DEUTCH. Will the gentleman yield for a second?

Mr. ROHRABACHER. You know, I can't do it, because I have limited time. But I will be happy to have the discussion with you on your time.

Mr. DEUTCH. I appreciate that.

Mr. ROHRABACHER. Let me ask you this: We have heard about the Russians today. The most important issue that came out of this whole, how do you say—this episode in American democracy was that the Russians had hacked into our systems and interfered with our election, and you all agreed that there was something to that.

The most important example of that was, that we could all understand, is that they hacked into the Democratic National Committee and got out all of those emails and made public what was in those emails. So the public had this information they wouldn't have otherwise had.

But let me ask you this: From a lot of other experts that I have read that they said it was impossible for the Russians to have been the ones to have done that, that it was probably done by an insider into the DNC, because the thumb drive that—where this information was downloaded was downloaded from someone on the inside rather than using the Internet, which would have taken a lot longer to get that same information.

Have you read anything about that? You are the experts. Is that an analysis that a group of retired intelligence officers have claimed is true? Do you think that is true, meaning that it was an inside job by what you can see with your expertise into cyberattacks?

Mr. PAINTER. So I will start by saying that you are right, hacking is not new. Influence operations are not new. However—and even—there was hacking back in 2008 into both the Republican and Democratic campaigns.

Mr. ROHRABACHER. You know, I have only got 5 minutes. Do you disagree with that?

Mr. PAINTER. The difference then was it was used to gather intelligence and not weaponized to try to affect our elections. You know, there are lots of——

Mr. ROHRABACHER. I have got to ask you about this—look. I am sorry. But it is my time right now. They are not going to give me 1 extra minute to get your answer.

Mr. Chairman, I ask unanimous consent for 1 extra minute to get them to answer.

Chairman ROYCE. No objection.

Mr. ROHRABACHER. All right.

Mr. Chairman, I think it is appalling—I think that type of camaraderie is appalling when we have a witness that is refusing to go to——

Chairman ROYCE. Okay. We go to Mr. Albio Sires of New Jersey.

Mr. SIRES. Thank you, Mr. Chairman. And thank you for being here today.

You know, I am one of those guys that is on a different scale here. I think that while we sleep, countries like Russia, China, North Korea, and Iran are plotting how to undermine this country. Especially Russia. So has America really woken up to the fact that this is a real danger to our country, or do we still need to go a little ways more to recognize how dangerous this is to our country?

Mr. Painter.

Mr. PAINTER. So, yes, I think we have not gone far enough. I think it should have been a wake-up call. There has been a lot of wake-up calls we have seen from a lot of different threats. The Sony Pictures hack by North Korea, some of the big data thefts. And the effect on our election. I think we need to have a sustained focus on this. This is not a blip. This is going to be repeated in the future. And so we absolutely have to sustain the focus on this in the future.

Mr. SIRES. Mr. Miller.

Mr. MILLER. I agree that absolutely we need more focus on, really, the full spectrum of cyber-related threats out there. We have certainly heard a lot already today about many of the very high profile hacks. And it is very important, a couple of features of those that have been pointed out already, you do have increasingly sophisticated threats and threat actors, including nation states increasingly involved in this activity. And then even when we do have bilateral agreements in some instances to not do a specific thing like hack for commercial purposes, the reality is, all these other cyber policies that are problematic that we have been talking about can really cause some of the very same issues, for instance, by just requiring companies to turn over source code or things like that. So it is a problem that we have to magnify.

Mr. SIRES. Mr. Sulmeyer.

Mr. SULMEYER. Yes, sir. It should be a wake-up call, not just about cyber operations and cybersecurity, but also about these information operations and the knowing introduction of fake and false information. Others tend to view that as a full spectrum activity to do in war and peace. We tend to think about information operations more in a wartime context. That is an important difference we should be conscientious of. Thank you.

Mr. SIRES. And in terms of places like Russia, they have become so sophisticated that they don't have to have their imprint in there, but they use hackers and criminal networks. Is that accurate?

Mr. PAINTER. Yeah. I mean, I think one of the concerns we have had for a long time is not just state actors on their own, but state actors using proxies. And they do that because it is more difficult to trace it to them, more difficult to attribute to them. That is a real concern as well. And so as we look at the spectrum of different threats, and it is the Annual Threat Report, in 2017 and also in many years before that, Russia, China North Korea, and Iran have been the key threat state actors, and Russia has been one of the most sophisticated.

Mr. SIRES. How do we respond to that?

Mr. Sulmeyer, how do——

Mr. SULMEYER. Gone are the days when the non-state actors were less capable. Non-state actors can be just as capable now as state actors. So the distinction in my mind is now moot.

In a number of situations, we need to hold the state accountable because the non-state actor is actually a proxy for the state. And when our Justice Department indicted several Russian criminals for the hack on Yahoo, there is a lot of good information in that indictment about that situation.

Mr. SIRES. So that tells me that diplomacy—they can easily get around that, whatever arrangements we make.

Mr. PAINTER. No. I mean, diplomacy is one of the tools in our tool set. I absolutely agree that law enforcement and stronger enforcement and giving the tools for that is important. That is what I used to do in one part of my career. Diplomacy is pressing not just the state that is responsible, but other states who are similarly victims of this conduct, to take action against a state that is doing it. And that is one of the things of deterrence we have to be much better at.

Mr. SIRES. Mr. Miller, do you have any response to that?

Mr. MILLER. Well, I think to go back to your previous question that I didn't answer about the different types of state actors. That is absolutely true that it is not just the state-sponsored cyber activities that we need to——

Mr. SIRES. And some states work with these hackers——

Mr. MILLER. Yeah. Yeah. Yeah. Absolutely. I think another feature of this problem is that it is also—it is not just economic rationales behind the hacking. Increasingly we see political or activist types of hacking as well from WikiLeaks, for instance, and others. And it is a really—it is a very complicated environment in that regard.

Mr. SIRES. My time ran out. Thank you.

Thank you, Mr. Chairman.

Chairman ROYCE. We go to Joe Wilson, South Carolina.

Mr. WILSON. Thank you, Mr. Chairman. And thank each of you for being here today.

Mr. Painter, in the fiscal year 2017 National Defense Authorization Act, Congress expanded the role of the Global Engagement Center to include countering foreign, state, and unsafe propaganda and disinformation efforts that threaten U.S. national security interests as well as the security interest of U.S. allied and partner nations.

With this expanded mission, could you please explain, or describe the role of the Global Engagement Center and the broader U.S. cyber diplomacy effort?

Mr. PAINTER. So the Global Engagement Center was a separate part of the State Department from where I was. We did talk to the Global Engagement Center. As I said previously, if we are really taking this seriously, and we are trying to combat all these threats, not just the terrorist threats, but also other states who are trying to influence various operations around the world, I think the Global Engagement Center can and should play an important role. And I think that that legislation helps ensure that, if it is properly resourced, if it is properly doing all the things it needs to do.

Mr. WILSON. And that really is the next point. Is there more that Congress can do to back up the Center?

Mr. PAINTER. I haven't been to the State Department now for a few months, so I can't say how it is operating currently. I would say that it is an important mission. It has got to be a mission that is done strategically. I think one of the problems we had in that space is if the government is simply saying it, we are not doing the best job, we have to get other interlocutors who have more credibility in the community doing that. That is one of the things the Global Engagement Center has and can continue to do. It is only part of the solution, though. We also have to work with social media companies and maybe create some sort of task force that I talked about before to deal with these issues more generally.

Mr. WILSON. We look forward to your input.

And, Mr. Miller, a persistent problem that has presented itself in cyberspace is attribution.

Could you please describe the process of attributing malicious activity in cyberspace and the technical and political challenges associated with attribution. What are the benefits or pitfalls of international attribution organization, and would all nations participate?

Mr. MILLER. Thank you for the question, Representative Wilson.

Absolutely, attribution is a really important piece of the equation here. I am not a technical expert. But by all accounts, we have gotten a lot better collectively at attribution in cyberspace. However, at least based on my knowledge, it is definitely not—it is still more—it is hard to have absolute 100 percent certainty in all cases in terms of attribution. As we have been describing, there is a whole host of cyber threat actors involved. Oftentimes there are various different ways to try to mask an IP address, or what have you, on the Internet. But I think your question does highlight the need for continuing to share cyber threat information and vulnerabilities with our partners and on other information, particularly partners internationally to really try to have as much information as we can to try to get the best information we can about tough issues, such as attribution.

Mr. WILSON. Thank you.

And, Dr. Sulmeyer, what is your view about attribution?

Mr. SULMEYER. Yes, sir.

Sophisticated states and companies can and do attribute. Just like anything, nothing is perfect. But gone are the days when attribution as a sort of bumper sticker—gone are those days when attribution was hard to do. It is a complicated process. You use all source methods of intelligence. You don't just rely on an IP address or cyber technical indicators. You throw everything at the book in trying to figure out who did it. And the critical part here is that now companies are in the mix as well, not just governments. And that muddies the water as well as for everyone.

Mr. WILSON. And, actually, Mr. Miller, you have already hit on this. But—and both of you, the potential of Russia and China working with us, and, of course, it seems inconceivable, but DPRK, any level of attribution from those particular countries?

Mr. MILLER. Well, to the extent you are asking about attribution from North Korea in particular, as I am sure you know, the Department of Homeland Security did, in fact, attribute the WannaCry attacks to North Korea right before the holidays. And I certainly, as Mr. Sulmeyer says, I think the U.S. or any nation state takes great pains before they publicly attribute. But when they do, I have a high degree of confidence that it is reliable information.

Mr. WILSON. Again, thank each of you for being here today.

Thank you, Mr. Chairman.

Chairman ROYCE. Thank you, Mr. Wilson.

Before we go to Congresswoman Karen Bass, I think we want her to get her full time, so might I suggest that we can—oh, we can go now.

All right. We go now to you. Afterwards, we will recess until the third vote, and come back immediately afterwards. Okay?

Congresswoman Karen Bass.

Ms. BASS. I appreciate that. Mr. Painter, could you please explain why the administration downgraded your office and what is the status of the office today?

Mr. PAINTER. So I don't know. We had a very good, I think, close working relationship with the people at the NSC with Rob Joyce, Tom Bossert and others. This is something where we were continuing to make progress on these issues.

Ms. BASS. So what were you told?

Mr. PAINTER. I think it was part of a larger reorganization where they were trying to get rid of all the special envoys, all the direct reports to the Secretary. I think, frankly, there was maybe a lack of understanding of the importance of this issue and how it fit into the——

Ms. BASS. Is it staffed today? Does the office exist?

Mr. PAINTER. So the office, as I understand it, my old office still exists. They have kept it together, which I think is critically important.

Ms. BASS. So who is staffing it?

Mr. PAINTER. My former deputy is still there, and several of the people who were just a great team are still there, and that is important.

Ms. BASS. So what are they doing?

Mr. PAINTER. They are working on some of these issues. They are continuing to work on it, however, the level of the person who is assigned over there is at a lower level, deputy assistant secretary level. He is in an economic reporting chain. As important as those issues are, it doesn't give full voice to all these other issues around deterrence, around incident response.

Ms. BASS. So what signal do you think that sends, especially to Russians and Chinese and other actors?

Mr. PAINTER. Look, quite frankly—and I have talked to a lot of our allies and others about this—I think it sends a message, as I said before, to our adversaries that this is an opportunity for them to flex their muscles and try to influence even more than they have the international debate. If we are not there in a leadership role, if it is a signal that this is not as important an issue in the State Department, and——

Ms. BASS. So if you take that combined with what is going on today in terms of the attacks on the FBI and the other intelligence agencies, what do you think is happening in preparation for our midterm?

Mr. PAINTER. I think we need to do everything we can, because the Russians will be there. Other actors could be there. If the goal is to sow chaos, which I think it is, you don't know which party is going to be affected. It is going to be something where they are going to come back, they are going to try to create chaos.

Ms. BASS. Do you think they see what is going on here as chaos today?

Mr. PAINTER. Well, I think what we see is that the people that we need to defend those networks, the FBI, who I have worked with and have tremendous respect for, the Department of Justice, who I used to work for and I have tremendous respect for, if we diminish their ability to fight these types of issues and our intelligence community that is shooting ourselves in the foot. We need to be able to deal with these issues.

Ms. BASS. Do you think we are not vulnerable today in terms of the midterm elections?

Mr. PAINTER. I can't make an assessment about the midterm elections themselves, except for to say if we don't take action, if we continue to not make this a high priority issue, and not communicate that this is a high priority issue, one that is really the top of the agenda and we will take action, and I talked about some of the actions we could take, including a clear declaratory statement and making sure we take actions——

Ms. BASS. So in addition to a declaratory statement, which I don't think we have done, what type of consequences do you think would stop, in particular, the Russians?

Mr. PAINTER. Look, it is hard to assess, but even if you impose consequences on the Russians, whether that will stop them, but it will at least make them think twice about it, and you can do economic sanctions to even greater ones than we have now. You can think about a whole range of options that we have in deterrence, not just economic. We can think about, you know, other law enforcement options. We can think about other options that we can pursue, but we need to be able to communicate that, too, saying we will do these things if you take these actions to try to make——

Ms. BASS. And last question. I know we need to go to votes. You made specific reference to legislation, and I was wondering if you could be more specific than that in terms of what bills you were talking about.

Mr. PAINTER. I know there are a bunch of bills, there are a couple in the House dealing—I think there is one dealing with sanctions; there is one with giving more tools to deter actions on the Senate side. There is a bill that will help protect election systems. So there are a lot of efforts out there. I think the most important thing is we make sure that the people who are trying to keep this from happening have the tools in place, and that we give the resources and ability to help work with local and state election officials to up their game and have better cybersecurity.

Ms. BASS. Thank you very much, Mr. Chairman.

Chairman ROYCE. Thank you very much, Congresswoman Bass, and so at this point we will recess. We will resume immediately following the third vote. We stand in recess.

[Recess.]

Chairman ROYCE. If I could have the attention of the witnesses and the other members, we are going to reconvene at this time, and we will go first to Mr. Ted Yoho of Florida and then to Mr. Bill Keating of Massachusetts with their questioning.

Mr. YOHO. Thank you, Mr. Chairman, I appreciate it and I appreciate you holding this hearing at this moment. And I think this is such a very important topic, the cybersecurity of the United States of America and around the world. And I have lost my note here. Hang on just a minute. Bear with me.

Chairman ROYCE. Well, as you search for that, I have just received a letter, if I could.

Mr. YOHO. Go ahead.

Chairman ROYCE. If you could yield me some time——

Mr. YOHO. Yes, sir.

Chairman ROYCE [continuing]. From the Secretary of State announcing that the Department is creating a Bureau for Cyberspace and Digital Economy headed by an assistant secretary. I ask unanimous consent that this be included in the record. I think this is a positive step, but we are going to continue to work with the Department and continue to work with our colleagues over on the Senate side to pass the legislation we have passed out of this committee to ensure that this assistant secretary of the Bureau is empowered to engage on the full range of cyber issues dealing with security and human rights and the economy. And with that I would like to yield back to the gentleman from Florida.

Mr. YOHO. Again, thank you, Mr. Chairman. I have been here for 6 years, and I remember some of the first meetings we had here in this committee. We started talking about a cybersecurity policy for the United States, and I found it shocking that the United States did not have a definition of what a cybersecurity threat was, how it was defined, if it was amount of life lost, money lost, or infrastructure shut down, like a power grid. And then we didn't have the response for that, which I found that much more shocking to allow us to tell other nations when they do something, what they can expect from us. I am currently working on legislation that would complement Chairman Royce's Cyber Diplomacy Act with a deterrent and response mechanism.

One limitation of U.S. cyber deterrence is that the United States, as I mentioned, does not have a formal process to name and shame perpetrators when they are identifiable. We have seen how effective naming and shaming can be in other contexts like the Annual Trafficking in Persons Report, or the list of state sponsors of terrorism. The goal here is not to shame people, but the goal here is to get people to be honest actors in the world we live in. And if people don't follow and respect other nations' rules and laws, you get a breakdown of society.

So my question to all three of you is do you think it would be helpful to create a designation for known malicious cyber actors, or what should a designation process for known malicious cyber actors look like? If you guys want to just kind of go down the panel, and I have got one more follow-up question if I have time.

Mr. PAINTER. I think it is an interesting idea. I think there are some things you have to be careful about, though. Even when the U.S. knows and can attribute the conduct, sometimes they want to make that public, and that is useful, as we did in the case of North Korea, as we recently did with North Korea again, Russia and some others and China. Sometimes you don't. Sometimes you want to use it as a tool to then go back privately to that country and tell them basically this is unacceptable as a predicate to doing more. So that is one issue.

The other issue, I would say, is that if I don't know the scope of the naming and shaming you are talking about, if it is for nonstate actors for, like, criminal activity that is coming from their country, one of the challenges there is sometimes those countries simply don't have the tools to deal with it.

Mr. YOHO. Let me ask Mr. Miller that, because I think you are the one that brought up that a lot of the proxy groups are working with state actors, I think that was you.

Mr. MILLER. Yes, sir.

Mr. YOHO. Your button, please.

Mr. MILLER. Sorry. Yes, sir, I did bring that up. And I think I would agree with that. We don't want to look at this too narrowly to only focus on the state actors, because they are working with a whole variety of others, so, to just amplify what Mr. Painter was saying, I think it is definitely an interesting idea, but we want to just proceed carefully because we don't want to put the focus on one area, and then have others kind of running free, if you will, and kind of leading to a false sense of security in that regard.

Mr. YOHO. Right. Dr. Sulmeyer?

Mr. SULMEYER. Congressman, I do agree. I find the idea interesting. The trick for me would be to balance between strategic ambiguity, and when you really want to articulate precisely what actions will trigger what responses. It is always a balance.

Mr. YOHO. And I think we need to do that, because right now there is not, and so there is so much ambiguity and gray areas that the obvious thing that countries are going to do is keep expanding that and pushing that. And what sort of consequence should the United States impose on groups that have committed attributable cyberattacks on the United States? And we already talked about the actors that are acting on their behalf. Mr. Painter?

Mr. PAINTER. We have to have a menu of options. Right now we have diplomatic options to bring pressure, not just by us, but by our allies and partners; we have economic things, like sanctions; we have law enforcement tools; we have cyber operational tools, which I think are sometimes often overrated; and we have kinetic tools, which we are unlikely to use in a cyber event, but——

Mr. YOHO. Go ahead.

Mr. PAINTER. So I think what we need to do is really expand our tool set, have more tools, work with partners to bring these consequences and do it in a more timely fashion.

Mr. YOHO. All right. I am out of time, and I thank you gentlemen for your patience.

Chairman ROYCE. We go to Mr. William Keating of Massachusetts.

Mr. KEATING. Thank you, Mr. Chairman. I would like to say again, thank our witnesses. It is great to have former officials; it is great to have counsels and think tanks; it is great to have people from facilities like the JFK School in my home State. But I would say, again, it is important to have actual members of the Trump administration here. It is important for our committee, and I mean that as no criticism to you, Mr. Chairman, because I know you have pushed for this, too, but the continued lack of having these people here is, at best, indifference, worst case, arrogance. So with that, I will get the attention of our witnesses and thank them for being here once again.

Mr. Painter, you have said that basically it is irrelevant, if I had my notes, what we do without a deterrent response, and you said that absent that response virtually it guarantees us a recurrence of this behavior, and the norm of inaction is a big deal. Now, the fact that we didn't move on the Russian sanctions will have an impact in that regard. We can't go back at their elections because in Russia, opponents either end up imprisoned or poisoned or dead or missing, but in our country, we are open to this.

I was very concerned, you know, with the public information that in 29 States it has been reported publicly, that Russians were actually in our voting apparatus. Can you tell us beyond just the bots and everything they are doing from, you know, to really change attitudes and use that kind of propaganda here, what about actually being involved in the voting apparatus? What dangers does that present? Any of you, but Mr. Painter, if, you could start.

Mr. PAINTER. It presents a real danger. Now, in some sense, the U.S. system has some resiliency because there are so many different states and jurisdictions that have their own ways of doing voting. On the other hand, you can imagine an attacker getting in, either not just changing voting machines, but also, doing things with respect to voter rolls and registrations and all kinds of other things that could, at the very least, create uncertainty and havoc during the election, and that is all you need to do, right?

You don't need to actually change a result. Creating uncertainty itself could delegitimize an election. So I think that is a huge issue. That is why we need to do everything we can also to work with the State and local authorities to protect their systems.

Mr. KEATING. Mr. Miller?

Mr. MILLER. Thank you. Yes, I would agree with that. Absolutely, on one of the other items. Potential threats to voting machines and voting systems highlights is just how, frankly, we are living in a world when we talk about the Internet of Things and other connected cyber physical devices where there are more and more attack vectors that we all need to protect both industry and government working together, so that further highlights the need for a well-functioning State Department, but it is not just the State Department that we are talking about here today. It is a bit of a cliche, but cyber is a team sport, and the Department of Homeland Security, to their credit, has been doing a lot of work on this topic.

Mr. KEATING. Thank you. I am just—on that subject I will interrupt, but I know Mr. Sulmeyer, his report is coming out in that regard that will be helpful, but you just mentioned homeland, and it is a whole of government approach to this. I am concerned of the threats to the grid that are there. We issued requirements that bolster our nuclear reactors, or nuclear power plants to make them stronger, more resilient against a cyberattack, yet the NRC alone, in my district, waived that requirement.

Now, don't you think that the NRC by themselves shouldn't be in that position? Shouldn't there be, if there is a whole-of-government approach, shouldn't there be input from the Department of Homeland Security, from State, from other entities of government?

Mr. PAINTER. Look, it is a classic risk management issue, right, and that is a high risk, very high impact if things happen, and I would say you need to be extraordinarily careful in how you do these things. And I think it would benefit from the intelligence community, from other communities in our Government that can pass on information so that can be a more reasoned decision.

Mr. KEATING. I have 30 seconds left, so I couldn't agree more. The NRC alone being able to do that without the input of our intelligence agencies makes no sense whatsoever, and I know, Mr. Sulmeyer, you wanted to get to that other question.

Mr. SULMEYER. Well, just to say, I think the principles are the same, which is, I don't want to bet the farm or deterrence. I would much rather make us much harder to hack and prevent the bad guy from being able to act. You can look at our play books for State and local officials to do that for elections. We should also be having the same facilities you described. Thank you.

Mr. KEATING. Thank you. I yield back.

Chairman ROYCE. We go to Mr. Tom Garrett of Virginia.

Mr. GARRETT. Thank you, Mr. Chairman. I would ask first, Mr. Miller, I presume, sir, you are an attorney?

Mr. MILLER. Yes, sir.

Mr. GARRETT. That is a yes-or-no question. Thank you. I don't have a lot of time.

Let me ask you this, would foreign interference in elections be easier if sensitive national security information was kept on a private server? That is a yes-or-no question, too, sir.

Mr. MILLER. You know, I——

Mr. GARRETT. Yes or no, sir. Mr. Painter, would foreign interference in elections be more difficult or less if sensitive information was kept on a private server?

Mr. PAINTER. It depends on the security of the server.

Mr. GARRETT. Okay. If it were a private server kept in the bathroom closet in a Denver loft, might that impact it? Would that be a highly secure server based on your training and experience? Mr. Sulmeyer, yes or no?

Mr. SULMEYER. I'm sorry, it does depend on the security setup of each server.

Mr. GARRETT. Okay. You guys are absolutely correct. And it shocks me, though, with your amazing credentials that when asked, Mr. Miller and Mr. Sulmeyer, if you are familiar with the United States interfering in foreign elections that you went, "Oh, I don't know," because the United States media has covered this extensively. In fact, Nina Agrawal in The Los Angeles Times December 21, 2016, wrote a story entitled, "The U.S. is no Stranger to Interfering in the Elections of Other Countries." Are any of you familiar with the U.S. interfering in the elections of other countries via open source information? Any of you, yes or no?

Okay. I am running out of time, gentlemen.

If someone kept information that was sensitive of a national security politically sensitive nature on a private server and they were found to have done such acts, would it be useful to punish that information to prohibit or prevent that sort of behavior in the future?

Okay. No yes or no answers there?

Okay. And if you heard that somebody had reached out from the United States Senate to a foreign power, say, I don't know, the Russians, and said, Will you work with me, I will help you get media opportunities, it is important to, and I quote, "counter the policies of this administration," would that be troubling?

Okay. No answers on that.

Would it be troubling if a member of this elected body had reached out to a foreign government, say, I don't know, the Russians, and said it is important to undermine his prospect for reelections. I will help you get contacts with the U.S. media, would that be troubling?

No answers.

Are any of you gentlemen familiar with the story in the London papers from 1992 detailing Senator Ted Kennedy's reaching out to the Russians to interfere in the 1984 elections? No? Okay.

Are any of you familiar with the nuclear freeze movement? Any of you? No? Okay.

Are any of you familiar with the funding mechanisms of the nuclear freeze movement and their activities in the United States Presidential elections? Would you be shocked to learn that the nuclear freeze movement was largely funded by the Soviet Union and that they worked against the Reagan elections in 1980 and 1984?

Crickets.

Mr. Chairman, I will yield back the balance of my time.

Mr. ROHRABACHER. Will the gentleman yield his time to——

Mr. GARRETT. Mr. Chairman, I take that back. I yield the balance of my time to my colleague, Mr. Rohrabacher.

Mr. ROHRABACHER. Thank you very much, and let me just note for the record, we have witnesses who are unable to give direct answers to things as important as this reflects on your integrity and—or your knowledge base. I don't know which. We will let whoever is looking at this decide.

Also let me know note that for 30 years, I have never turned down a colleague when he asked for an extra minute in a situation like we had earlier. That discourtesy is unfortunate, Mr. Chairman, as you have tried to develop a bipartisan camaraderie here, even when you ask tough questions like what we just heard, and I think that should give us all a little something to think about.

Let me note also for the record, Mr. Painter intentionally used time that was allocated to finding a truth in order to obscure the dissemination of information based on a question by a Member of Congress.

Mr. CICILLINE. Mr. Chairman, I would ask that order be maintained in this committee that the integrity of these witnesses not be impugned, and that Mr. Rohrabacher doesn't speak for this committee when he makes that kind of assessment.

Mr. GARRETT. Mr. Chairman, I yielded my time to Mr. Rohrabacher, and I would ask that he be granted the time taken by this gentleman to whom I did not yield time.

Chairman ROYCE. There are 50 seconds remaining in the time.

Mr. ROHRABACHER. I also find it absolutely unforgivable that another member would use limited time to interfere with a member's right to ask a very pertinent question. Now, and we have 30 seconds, so I will ask you the yes-or-no question that you refused to answer before. Is it more likely when knowing that as has been reported by people who are retired intelligence officers, that it is highly unlikely that the Russians could have been the ones who hacked into the Democratic National Committee and made those emails public, that instead, it was highly likely that it was an inside job, yes or no?

Mr. PAINTER. Sir, I do not accept that.

Mr. ROHRABACHER. Okay. Fine. You won't—what about you?

Mr. MILLER. I am not exactly sure about your question honestly.

Mr. ROHRABACHER. Okay. What about you? So we have witnesses today who can't say anything that would be damaging to the Democratic Party or to one side of this argument. Shame on you.

Mr. PAINTER. Sir, to be clear, I am concerned about any interference by——

Mr. ROHRABACHER. You do not have the floor.

Chairman ROYCE. Time has expired. All time has expired. We go now to Mr. David Cicilline of Rhode Island.

Mr. CICILLINE. First of all, I want to apologize to these witnesses that you were just subjected to that discourteous behavior, and I certainly want to applaud you for your integrity, your candor today, your service to our country. And I would like to begin, it is one thing to be unwilling to respond to foreign interference in our elections in cyberattacks in particular, but it is quite another thing to speak in a way, and to describe Russian interference in our elections as a hoax, as fake news to discredit intelligence agencies that have done this work, have fired the FBI Director because of the Russia thing.

So my question is, how does the behavior like that undermine our efforts to protect our democracy and protect us from these kinds of cyberattacks? Does it enhance it, or does it make it more difficult, Mr. Painter?

Mr. PAINTER. Look, as I said before, I think we have to be very clear that this is a huge issue, and that we are not going to countenance this happening again. I think some of the things I outlined about what we should be doing about this needs to focus on the future, too, because this is going to happen again. I think we need to be clear and clear-eyed of how important and how big an issue this was and that this is something that is not acceptable. The intelligence community has concluded this in both administrations.

Mr. CICILLINE. And is it important to have a strong declaration from the leader of the country that says this will not be tolerated, we will make certain there are consequences if you do this again, and create some national commitment to protect our democracy and our electoral institutions?

Mr. PAINTER. Yes, that is the kind of declaratory statement I was talking about earlier.

Mr. CICILLINE. Mr. Miller, do you agree that that is necessary?

Mr. MILLER. I think I absolutely agree that the types of policies that are expressed in the Cyber Diplomacy Act should be loudly broadcast. You know, everything we have been talking about, keeping the Internet open and free, secure, et cetera.

Mr. CICILLINE. Dr. Sulmeyer?

Mr. SULMEYER. Yes, I agree.

Mr. CICILLINE. Thank you. So with respect to kind of what we are doing to respond to this very real threat, CIA Director Pompeo said there is no question the Russians are coming back in another attempt to interfere with our democratic institutions, which, as you say, should not be a Republican or Democratic issue, it is an issue that is important to every single American in our country.

When we had the Attorney General before us, he said, and I quote, "I have not followed through to see where we are on that," referring to an effort to review our practices and our policies and legislative infrastructure to support our democratic institutions. And he said very candidly, "Are we at the level we need to be at? I don't think so." Are you aware of any effort underway by our Government, by the administration, to prevent a reoccurrence of foreign interference by a foreign adversary in our elections in 2018?

Mr. PAINTER. I am not aware of any high-level effort. That is why I am saying that time is running out, and this is an issue that we need to take seriously. And I think there are certainly a lot of professionals in the government that are looking at this issue with the FBI and the intelligence agencies, and really across the government. I think this needs to be a top priority.

Mr. CICILLINE. Mr. Miller, are you aware of any high-level effort coordinated at the administration to respond to this very real threat in the elections which are only 10 months away?

Mr. MILLER. It is difficult to comment on the level, per se, sir, but I am aware, I do a lot of work with the Department of Homeland Security. I do know the Department of Homeland Security is very much focused on this threat and working operationally, for instance, with the States and others to try to help.

Mr. PAINTER. And I would agree with that. I have seen that, too.

Mr. CICILLINE. Dr. Sulmeyer?

Mr. SULMEYER. I would reiterate Mr. Miller's point about DHS, but no in a broader national coordinated level, no.

Mr. CICILLINE. And I think I just would like to conclude by making reference to what Mr. Keating said. It would be very useful to actually hear from administration officials and allow the world to hear in a very strong declarative statement, not only that they acknowledge that this happened, but their commitment to be certain that it never happens again, and that they are working in an interagency way to ensure that that happens. I would love to hear from members of the administration before our committee to actually talk about that.

The final thing I want to ask you about is, we passed the Countering America's Adversaries Through Sanctions Act recently, and we, of course, learned that the administration has failed to implement the sanctions that we imposed as a direct result of Russian aggression and Russian interference in our elections.

Some people have tried to explain that away and just said, well, just the threat of doing that has been a deterrent, but, of course, it was also to punish them for interfering in American elections. What is the impact of the failure of the administration not to implement these sanctions against Russia, both in terms of their behavior and what kind of message it sends to the rest of the world?

Mr. PAINTER. So I don't discount that the threat could have an effect, as it did with the Chinese in bringing them to the table. However, this is a huge issue, and the fact that we haven't done it yet, and I know there is some confusion about whether we will do it in the future, we need to take action. We need to make sure there are consequences. Without consequences, there is not deterrence, and there is an invitation to do it again.

Mr. SULMEYER. I would just say it risks emboldening our adversaries very much.

Mr. CICILLINE. Thank you.

Chairman ROYCE. We go now to Ann Wagner of Missouri.

Mrs. WAGNER. Thank you, Mr. Chairman, for your leadership on the issue. I was disturbed last month when China's civil aviation regulator demanded an apology from Delta Airline for listing Taiwan as a country on the Delta Web site. Also last month, China blocked Marriott Web sites and intimidated the country into groveling and apologizing for listing both Taiwan and Tibet as separate countries. China's actions are egregious of violations of basic expressions and speech. They were also part of coordinated efforts to undermine regional stability.

Just a couple weeks ago, China unilaterally announced that it would open disputed air routes through the Taiwan Strait. My colleagues and I wrote a letter to the Chinese Ambassador calling on China to enter into a constructive dialogue with Taiwan. It is entirely inappropriate for China to use cyber retaliation against American companies to push its political agenda and aggression against Taiwan, and the administration should be responding to this, I believe, at the highest level.

Mr. Painter, in 2014, Congress authorized the administration to sanction foreign persons that commit cyber espionage. What progress has the administration made in sanctioning Chinese actors that repeatedly steal American IP?

Mr. PAINTER. Thank you for that question. About that same time, I think, the administration also came out with an Executive order listing sanctions for the first time that would apply to cyber activities, a range of cyber activities, including the activities you described. And I think that the fact that those sanctions were in place were indeed one of the things, among others, that drove the Chinese to come to the table and after for a long time, saying there was no difference between normal intelligence gathering, and taking trade secrets to benefit your commercial sector for a long time saying there was no difference at all and they didn't do either of them saying there was a difference and they agreed not to do the latter. And I think that was a landmark thing that was then replicated at the G20. Australia has reached an agreement with them; Germany has reached an agreement; the U.K. reached an agreement, that is important.

Now, I do agree with you——

Mrs. WAGNER. But what progress has been made, I guess, is what I am concerned about, because it is my sense, to be perfectly honest, that both the Obama and the Trump administrations have kind of shied away from using that authority?

Mr. PAINTER. Look, I think that has to be a tool in your tool kit. And I think you have to be ready and willing to use it, and as I said earlier, sanctions were not taken off the table when that agreement was reached. If there is a violation, if that agreement is violated, that has to be one of the tools and should be one of the tools that is used. I would say that that sanctions order from back in 2014 or 2013 has been underused. I think we need to use that as one of our tools more aggressively and in the right cir-

cumstances, not just with China, but with others, when we see conduct——

Mrs. WAGNER. Thank you.

Mr. PAINTER [continuing]. That rises to a certain level.

Mrs. WAGNER. Thank you for that testimony, because I believe it has been underutilized also.

Mr. Miller, 2 years ago Congress created a private right of action for victims of trade secret theft in U.S. courts. Have companies doing business in China begun taking advantage of this cause of action?

Mr. MILLER. Thank you for the question. I am actually really not aware of whether or not there have been a number of cases filed under that cause of action.

Mrs. WAGNER. I was just wondering if there are examples of companies bucking the trend of referring not to report or remedy losses?

Mr. MILLER. I do know that certainly, ITI's companies take intellectual property rights very seriously and, as I mentioned earlier, it is concerning that some of the government policies that we see around the globe that put U.S. companies, or any company's intellectual property——

Mrs. WAGNER. Relatedly, would you recommend that the Department of Justice direct additional resources toward prosecuting trade secret theft?

Mr. MILLER. Trade secret theft is—I mean, I think I would, yes, sure.

Mrs. WAGNER. Just they put forward this private right of action 2 years ago, we did here in Congress, and I just don't see it utilized, and I see harm coming to many of our companies.

Mr. Sulmeyer, in my brief time left, I believe that Russia issued a requirement that would force companies to submit the locations of data centers and servers to Russia's ICT regulators. Is this a security concern given that hackers and other malintentioned actors might know where to look for important data?

Mr. SULMEYER. Thank you, Congresswoman. Yes, I do believe that would be one among many security concerns that the regulators there enforce on companies, yes.

Mrs. WAGNER. Outrageous. Mr. Chairman, I believe my time has expired. I yield back.

Chairman ROYCE. Joaquin Castro of Texas.

Mr. CASTRO. Thank you, Chairman. Mr. Painter, as the chairman noted, the State Department just announced it plans to establish a new Bureau for Cyberspace and Digital Economy. Although elevating the issue of cyber diplomacy is positive, it strikes me as odd that the Bureau would report to the Under Secretary for Economic Growth, Energy, and the Environment rather than the Under Secretary for Political Affairs. Would the new Assistant Secretary be able to focus on a full range of cybersecurity and other critical issues under this arrangement?

Mr. PAINTER. I quite agree with you. I think that that is not the ideal arrangement. I think the Under Secretary for Economic Affairs, by their title and their responsibilities, really has to have that economic perspective. That is an important perspective to be sure, but if you look at all these issues, as I talked about in my written testimony, that include hard issues of security deterrence, incident response, issues around cyber operations and military actions in cyberspace, that does not fit close to in that substantive rubric. So you really need something really broad-based. I think the committee's recommendation to be under the Under Secretary of Political Affairs makes a lot more sense. It is a neutral reporting chain. They can deal with security issues, human rights issues that also don't fit.

There are sometimes conflicts between human rights issues and economic issues, for instance, and security issues and economic issues. You want a place where you can have full voice of all those issues, particularly the security issues that are really facing us today. And so I would say that I applaud the fact that they have taken action. I think it is great they are elevating it. That is exactly what should be done, but it would not put it under the Under Secretary for Economic Affairs. I would put it, at a minimum, under the Under Secretary for Political Affairs, where you can have full force of these issues.

Mr. CASTRO. No, thank you. And let me ask you three gentlemen, whoever wants to answer. Besides sitting on the Foreign Affairs Committee, I am also on the Intelligence Committee, so as you know, we have had, for over a year now, a front row seat in understanding how Russian hacking and basic cyber operations has affected our democracy. But the threats, as we mentioned in the committee, come not only from them but other nations, and non-state actors. So one of the issues that I have been working on, and I know others have also, is the eventual development of mutual cyber defense treaties.

Right now, you know, you think about the existence of NATO, for example, which mostly involves mutual defense when there is a physical intrusion of one country against another. You know, in your vision of the future, what is the future for any kind of mutual response to cyberattacks and cyber intrusions, if there is one?

Mr. PAINTER. Look, I think that is paramount actually. I think that as we look at sharpening our deterrence tools, one of the things we need to do is work with like-minded partners who can act together to sanction bad actors in cyberspace, and whether it is done by a treaty or it is a loose arrangement, which I think might be more flexible and valuable in this case, like we did with, for instance, the Proliferation Security Initiative, or in money laundering other areas, which I think probably may have worked better in the short term; that is important. I can also say that some bilateral arrangements, like with Australia and others, on larger defense issues, we have added cyber to that and said mutual defense treaties with those organizations would also involve cyber, and NATO has stepped up their game on cyber, including in the last summit, declaring it our domain.

Mr. SULMEYER. I would just say, I think it is a great idea, Congressman, to be pushing those kinds of arrangements. I would try to distinguish at times between when the treaty would come into effect during a crisis, and in steady state, and I wouldn't want to just reserve it for when things get hot. I would want to make sure that the information sharing that is happening on a steady-state basis, so you never have to really invoke the ones in a crisis.

Mr. MILLER. Just to briefly add to those comments of both my fellow witnesses, which I agree with, I absolutely think it is a good idea. It is clear we need all the tools in the tool shed, as Mr. Painter testified earlier, and multilateral agreements and vehicles are really important, and, you know, as well as the work that has been done in NATO certainly at a higher level. There have been some good agreements made in these areas at the G7 and G20, and then also, if you look at other tools like the Budapest Convention on Cyber Crime, for instance, there are ways to work together on these issues.

Mr. CASTRO. And it just it strikes me right now as a big gap or void in our defense, really, that this is not fully fleshed out essentially, that there is no kind of comprehensive agreement among friendly nations, at least, or even strong bilateral agreements to take—on a mutual cyber response and what exactly—when you would respond, and how you would respond, whether that involves private companies, for example, in the United States. So my time is up, but thank you, gentlemen, for your testimony.

Chairman ROYCE. If the gentleman would yield, I want to make it clear, we passed legislation to direct what Mr. Joaquin has suggested here, to direct that change in law and that bill is in the Senate, and we are going to continue to engage with the Department on who this new Assistant Secretary reports to.

However, the Department has made clear that this position will handle national security issues, so I want to point that out, including national security level cyber incidents, and promotion and adoption of a national process and programs that enable foreign territorial cyber threat detention, prevention, and response, and build foreign capacity to protect the global network.

So I think that with respect to the legislation we have moved into the Senate, we are starting to see a movement, and I especially thank the members of this committee for their engagement on this issue here today. We now go to Congresswoman Norma Torres of California.

Mrs. TORRES. Thank you, Mr. Chairman, and I want to begin by thanking our panelists for being here. Although I wasn't here during the earlier discussion, I want to tell you that this committee really prides itself from working on a bipartisan way, and we often truly enjoy the folks in the dialogue we have with our guests, so I apologize. It is not reflective of the entire committee. Certainly it is not reflective of me, and I am eager to hear your feedback on the issues that I am going to cover.

According to the Freedom House in 2017, freedom on the net report, governments around the world have dramatically increased their efforts to manipulate information on social media. We have seen this in our own hemisphere, Guatemala, for example, there are armies of paid trolls who are actually working to discredit the fight against corruption in the country.

I don't know if they are tied to the government or not, but they are called net centers, and they are working to undermine the work that we are doing in that country, and we have significant U.S. assistance in that country in the northern triangle of Central America. So how do you get more information about these net centers and other paid trolls, and how do we find out who is actually paying for them? And how do we push back on those efforts?

Mr. PAINTER. I mean, I think that information involves, for instance, working with our posts around the world in those countries, and with the intelligence community as well, and the law enforcement community. I think the way we push back is—I am concerned. I follow Freedom House's reports, and I think over time freedom online has been challenged around the world and this is a huge issue, and we have seen it by repressive regimes and we have seen it increasing in other places, as well.

And so, there are a number of things I think we can do. Our democracy and human rights part of the State Department does a number of grants around the world to promote freedom online, and also to protect dissidents and others and their own cybersecurity. There is something called the Freedom Online Coalition that the U.S. was a founding member of, which is I forget how many states it is now, it is over 30 that are around the world who value freedom online and deal with these issues and mutually come up with really good policies on these issues, and this is an issue I think is ripe for that. They have looked at things like network shutdowns and other issues in this space.

So I think we really—and one of the things that we used to do in the State Department is that we would raise freedom online in all of our bilateral discussions with other countries. And we would have these all-of-government discussions and I would have someone from our democracy and human rights there to talk about these issues. We need to continue to do that. This is a big deal. We need to make sure security is not used as a proxy by countries to overtake basic freedoms like freedom online, so that has to be part of our policy.

Mr. MILLER. Thank you, Congresswoman. To that, I would add, we have certainly appropriately talked a lot about the security policy and security challenges here today, and during this hearing. You know, and I think few would question, again, the important economic element of a lot of what we are talking about here today, particularly cross-border data flows, but I think your question highlights another really key element of, you know, frankly the Cyber Diplomacy Act, and also what we are talking about, which is these norms and values that this country supports of a free and open Internet, we have a First Amendment, free speech, privacy. All these issues are really important as well, and that is why it is so important to have the State Department and other U.S. Government entities out there internationally trying to influence the rest of the global community toward that way of thinking, because it is under assault in a lot of different ways.

Ms. TORRES. All right. It is a free and open Internet, and we absolutely want to continue to have that, but it is a free and open Internet for people, not necessarily for trolls or paid trolls.

Mr. MILLER. Sure, absolutely I would agree with that.

Ms. TORRES. I think my time is almost up, so I am not going to go into the next question. Thank you.

Chairman ROYCE. Thank you, Congresswoman. We will go to Brad Schneider of Illinois.

Mr. SCHNEIDER. Thank you, Chairman Royce. Thank you for having this meeting, and I just want to take a moment to thank you for your longstanding commitment and dedication to the bipartisanship within this committee and the commitment to work together, and I mention that in the context of what I feel was an outrageous and unjustified attack on our witnesses.

I appreciate you being here and sharing with us your perspectives. I am grateful for the work you have done and continue to do, and I hope that we don't see what we saw again. And thank you for talking about the increasingly important topic of cybersecurity. I have said this before in this committee, but it is too important not to repeat again. The U.S. intelligence agencies found that Russia did, in fact, interfere in the 2016 Presidential election, and there is no doubt in my mind that they will do it again, but it is not just me saying this. Last July, the Director of National Intelligence, Daniel Coats, said there was no dissent, I will repeat, no dissent inside the United States intelligence agencies about the conclusion that Russia used hacking and fake news to interfere in our election.

And just last month, the CIA Director Mike Pompeo stated, he believes Russia would seek to do so again. I will quote him: "I have every expectation they will continue to try and do that."

I share that, and just to lift two statements from the prepared testimony that the witnesses shared with us, Mr. Painter, you said, The U.S. did not foresee the hybrid threat posed by Russia's cyber-enabled attempt to undermine and influence the 2016 election that goes to the core of our democracy. I think that is critical. This is the foundation of our democracy, and every American should have the right to know that their vote will be counted, and that the integrity of their vote and the vote as a whole will be protected.

And, Dr. Sulmeyer, you noted that deterring a repeat of this conduct must be a priority for the entire United States Government, and, indeed, for all nations whose elections are susceptible to Russian interference, and I couldn't agree more. Unfortunately, this administration has not acted to secure our election systems and has not acted to punish those responsible for the 2016 meddling.

This administration is leaving the door open for Russia to interfere again. This is not just horrifying, it is unacceptable. Congress passed, and the President signed into law, the Countering America's Adversaries Through Sanctions Act, yet the administration has ignored the law by not imposing the strong sanctions laid out by CAATSA.

That is why I continue to raise the alarm regarding the seriousness of this situation, and why I join together with my colleague, former chairman Ileana Ros-Lehtinen of this committee, chairman of the subcommittee, to introduce the Defending Elections from Threats By Establishing Redlines, or the DETER Act. This bill would make clear that there will be consequences for those who interfere in our elections, and would ensure the United States Government had an actual strategy to prevent such interference. So I would like to ask the witnesses today a number of questions. First, what do you believe Putin hopes to achieve by interfering in our democratic process, and to what degree of certainty do you believe he will seek to do so in the elections coming up in November?

Mr. PAINTER. My sense, and I think what the intelligence community has said, too, is that to sow chaos, distrust, to undermine democratic systems, both here and around the world. That is, I think, the ultimate goal. And I think the likelihood this is going to happen in 2018, and also around the world, is incredibly high. There is no reason it wouldn't happen.

Mr. SCHNEIDER. Mr. Miller?

Mr. MILLER. I don't see any evidence to suggest that it is not likely to happen again for sure.

Mr. SCHNEIDER. Thank you. Dr. Sulmeyer?

Mr. SULMEYER. I think the motive is for Putin to increase his and Russia's relative power. That is why they are doing what they are doing, and yes, it seems inevitable they will do it again.

Mr. SCHNEIDER. And to some extent, do you have a sense that the administration's failure to respond is likely to embolden the Russians, and embolden Putin in their efforts to undermine our democracy?

Mr. PAINTER. Yes. I think we need to be strong. We need to be clear about what the consequences are. Whether that deters them or not, I don't know, but we need to be as clear as we can about that because it is likely to happen again.

Mr. SCHNEIDER. Dr. Sulmeyer, I think you were going to say something.

Mr. SULMEYER. Yes, we have to, but we can't rely on it, and that is why my colleagues at the Belfer Center have tried to go about helping state and local officials protect themselves as much as possible.

Mr. SCHNEIDER. Okay. And we are 9 months away from the election, 9 months from tomorrow. What should the administration be doing, what more can we do to help make sure that every vote will count, that every American knows that the integrity of their vote will be protected?

Mr. PAINTER. So I outlined some of these earlier, but one of them is exactly what Mr. Sulmeyer said. Working with the State and local authorities and DHS is doing some of this, but really upping that game to protect those systems to make sure they are secure. That is a technical part. Convening an interagency group at a high level to really focus on this; wherever it is coming from, whether it is Russia or other countries that we can really deal with this; enhancing our deterrence posture and tools we can use for deterrence; and coming up with a really strong declaratory message about what the problems are, what the consequences will be for doing this. And finally, I think working as has been happening, but working with social media and others to make sure that we are trying to cut off those areas of attack.

Mr. SCHNEIDER. Mr. Miller?

Mr. MILLER. I would focus again on DHS and the role that they play there. Again, as has been mentioned a few times, they are working with local officials, and that is absolutely important. It is also very important, DHS is kind of on the front lines of the public-private partnership between industry and working with industry partners and also, some of the things that stretch beyond this issue, like sharing threat information between the government and

industry to try to figure out what is happening, and avoid it is really important.

Mr. SCHNEIDER. I have gone well past my time. Thank you again
for your testimony today. Chairman, thank you for having this
hearing. I hope we will continue to focus on this very important
issue. I yield back.

Chairman ROYCE. Thank you. And our last questioning comes
from Mr. Brad Sherman of California.

Mr. SHERMAN. I want to build on the gentleman from Illinois'
questioning. It is always nice to have an office, give it importance,
give it the highest possible title. But if we are not serious about
cybersecurity, it is just an office. We know that Russia cyber
hacked for the purpose of affecting our election. And Congress
acted. Congress passed CAATSA, and every section of it that is
mandatory is ignored. So one wonders why create offices if the executive branch—I mean, why are we here? It is much warmer back
in California. I am here to try to legislate. We pass laws and the
President just ignores them, so let's go through. CAATSA Section
225 says, "The President shall impose sections on those who invest
in certain deep or Arctic oil locations with Russia provided a September 1, 2017, deadline." Nothing was done.

Then we have the bank transactions with especially designated
nationals. No bank has been sanctioned for a significant transaction with a Russian specially designated national. That is Section
226 of CAATSA. But of greatest concern is Section 231, because on
this one, we know what the administration is going to do. They
have said officially we refuse to follow the statute, because our oath
to the Constitution means nothing, and frankly, Congress means
nothing. Because that law says that there have to be sanctions
against those who do business with Russia's defense and intel com-
plexes.

Now, it does have a waiver provision, also ignored by the administration. What do they do? They issue a press release basically
saying, Congress, thanks for passing the law that says we shall do
something. We have determined it is unnecessary. We are not
going to do it.

This is something that I think the Russians would understand.
Their Duma is pretty much an advisory body. When it was initially
created, it was an advisory body to the czar, and I feel that perhaps
we should adjust the pay here to be no higher than that of the
1905 Duma, since our legislation has no more effect or legislative
actions.

And I will ask any of the witnesses, how are we going to have
an effective person in the State Department working on cyber
issues if we have a policy of not doing anything when the most
vital parts of our country are attacked through a cyber hack? Mr.
Painter?

Mr. PAINTER. So structure is important, but you are quite right,
structure alone doesn't solve the problem. You have to have structure——

Mr. SHERMAN. Structure can actually make the problem worse by
disguising the fact that you are doing nothing about the problem.

Mr. PAINTER. Structure is not the only thing. You need a good structure to actually lead this and communicate to the rest of the world it is important. However, you also need——

Mr. SHERMAN. I think we have communicated to the world that is not important.

Mr. PAINTER. But you are quite right. You need strong policies to actually enforce this and make sure that when you have attacks on this—alleged attacks or other attacks too, that there are consequences for those actors. And part of that is deterrence, but part of that is responding to incidents, and we need to do this. I hope this new Bureau actually does this, and is empowered to do this and that is going to be important.

Mr. SHERMAN. Okay. Now, you served as the State Department's Coordinator for Cyber Issues running an office that was eliminated days before you were scheduled to testify before the committee last summer. A lower level office was created in its stead. What did we lose by actually going backward on this rather than forward?

Mr. PAINTER. Look, I am heartened that the State Department has seen to provide a higher level structure. That is great. Again, I have problems about where it reports, given the range of issues it involves, because people are prisoners of their perspective, quite frankly, and someone who is an economic Under Secretary is going to be in that perspective. However, we had a lot of momentum going, and to say for a 6-month period or longer, that this was not, or communicate this is not a high priority, has an effect both with our adversaries and with our friends, and I don't understand why we did that. I think when we have a strategy in place to make even higher up, great, but why interrupt that in the interim?

Mr. SHERMAN. Unless you want to signal to the world and to Moscow that it isn't important. Look, I am a cosponsor of H.R. 3776, the Cyber Diplomacy Act. We passed this in the House. I think it had overwhelming support. We need U.S. international engagement on these cyber issues but just boxes in the State Department chart don't accomplish anything if you are not willing to take action. I yield back.

Chairman ROYCE. Let me just clarify that the administration has taken steps to implement CAATSA. They have briefed staff on both sides of the aisle at this point. Let me just make this point on their approach, which—and this is the point I want to make. Instead of sanctioning our allies that buy Russian weapons, what they are doing, at this point, is pressuring those allies to wind down those sales. I just want that understood.

Mr. SHERMAN. If the gentleman will yield.

Chairman ROYCE. But of course.

Mr. SHERMAN. First of all, law is law. You can't say we are going to violate the law because we have got a better deal to achieve your purpose.

Chairman ROYCE. I understand that in terms of their briefing with our staff here, they understand, or they articulate that this complies with the letter and spirit of the law as they now implement—without going through a whole debate in terms of what was laid out in the law and their methodology I am just explaining.

Mr. SHERMAN. Well, Turkey is going to give $2.5 billion to the military complex of Russia, and they are not going to be sanctioned, and we are going to be told that the fact that you have passed a law doesn't matter. We are not even going to even look at the waiver provisions of the law. We are going to ignore the law, and we have got a better idea and we are smarter than Congress, and trust us, we are there on your side, but we are going to ignore your legislation.

The fact is, I think Turkey fully understands they can send $2.5 billion to the Russians and to their military complex, and nothing will be done by this administration, except they will tell us privately and publicly that they know better, and that they are really on our side and they are really going to achieve our purposes.

Chairman ROYCE. Let me just add—reclaiming my time—it is up, the way it is written it is up to the administration to determine what constitutes a significant transaction, but they have also made clear to us in their discussions, that these designations are forthcoming. So I am just, for the record, clarifying those points.

I do know——

Mr. SHERMAN. If you will yield for just a second. If the administration wants to go public and say $2.5 billion from Turkey is not a significant transaction, let them have the guts to do so in public. I yield back.

Chairman ROYCE. And with that, I think we should go to our remaining member here with questions, and I am going to, at this point, give Mike McCaul the chairman's chair here, since I am supposed to be in the Financial Services Committee at this moment with Secretary Mnuchin. I thank all of our witnesses for their patience today especially given the votes that we had across the building. Thank you.

Mr. MCCAUL [presiding]. Let me recognize myself. And I chair the Homeland Security Committee, but I really enjoy being on this committee. It is a great intersection of similar issues, and cyber is really one of them, and I think I have done a lot on Homeland in terms of legislation, and I think at the State Department, and Chris Painter and I go way back at DOJ.

Cyber is a mission I would like to see elevated at the State Department. It is the only Department that can work with other countries to establish rules of the road, if you will, where we exist in a world where there are no, as you mentioned, real consequences to a lot of these cyber events that we have been discussing. And I just want to bring up one because I think it involves probably all three of you and myself, and that is the breach of 20 million security clearances at OPM where they stole mine, and I am sure Mr. Painter's and our fingerprints and all that. Were there any consequences to that breach, Mr. Painter?

Mr. PAINTER. I think there were. There were a lot of things said during that, after that. I think one of the problems there is espionage every country around the world does intelligence gathering. If that is classic espionage, if that is what that was, that is harder to deter, quite frankly, because every government other—you are not going to have an agreement not to actually do intelligence gathering with other countries. But at the same time, that doesn't change the fact that we need to harden our targets as much as possible, and when that happens, we don't have to like it either, we can do things in response to it.

Mr. McCaul. I know in 2015, the—maybe one thing that there was a meeting I think that was the only thing I saw take place but between the United States and China, and China agreed to refrain from conducting or supporting cyber-enabled theft of intellectual property, including trade secrets and other confidential business information, and I think I know the answer to this question but is China abiding with that agreement currently?

Mr. Painter. I think, to some extent, the jury is out. I think a lot of the people who track this in the private sector said there was a large diminution in that kind of activity. It doesn't mean that intrusions from China stopped, by my means. It means that kind of commercial espionage to benefit their commercial sector, which is something we don't do, we don't think any country should do, and they agreed not to do diminished substantially.

Now, there are have been mixed reports recently about that. I think if there is a breach of that agreement we have to take it seriously and we have to make sure there are consequences for that, but I think it did, at least, have an effect, and it was then enshrined in the G20 statement and with other countries around the world, so there was pressure not just from us, but from other countries too because they were also victims of this.

Mr. McCaul. Like in any agreement, I mean, what are the penalties for violating that agreement?

Mr. Painter. Yes, I mean the penalties, like I said, nothing was taken off the table. We didn't say, Hey, if you agree to this, we are not going to sanction you. We didn't give anything for that, right, so those are all still on the table. If we see that happening the government can use sanctions. The government can use, you know, other law enforcement actions like they have before against the PLA officers. There is still a range of things that the U.S. can do and the U.S. and its allies can do in appropriate circumstances, and you want to make sure you have the right factual basis to do that.

Mr. McCaul. In the——

Mr. Painter. I would submit, however, as I said before, I think our tool set is still too slim. I any we need to develop other tools to respond to these kinds of threats in cyberspace.

Mr. McCaul. Do you agree that if a NATO country was attacked in an act of cyber warfare, that Article 5 would apply and be invoked?

Mr. Painter. I absolutely do. In fact, NATO said that that was a fact. I mean, Article 5 is a fact-specific, case-by-case basis. It has been invoked once on 9/11, but I think if it is a sufficient attack that causes the same kind of death and injury that a physical one did, absolutely it could be involved in a case-by-case basis.

Mr. McCaul. The Russian interference in our elections, Congress passed sanctions on Russia for that. Were there any other consequences taken by the administration for that, and I got briefed by Jeh Johnson and DNI Clapper during the previous administration on that around October before the elections occurred. It was clear to me it was happening. The attribution was clear. I didn't see—my advice was to call it out for what it was, and that there should be consequences to bad behavior like that.

Mr. PAINTER. I would agree that the consequences should be imposed. There were a number of them in December at the end of the administration. There was some economic sanctions. There were throwing a number of diplomats out of the country and closing compounds. There were a number of things done. But for deterrence to actually work, it has to be timely, and 6 months later is a long time, and that has to continue because the threat is still there.

So I think the cyber community didn't really understand the nature of this threat. We knew about attacks against infrastructure. We knew about potential theft of intellectual property. We weren't focused on this hybrid threat when it happened.

Mr. McCAUL. Well, I have been working on my committee, Homeland. DHS will be—as we go into 2018 elections, there is no question that they are going to try to do this again.

Mr. PAINTER. Yes.

Mr. McCAUL. In fact, there is some evidence they are already interfering in some U.S. Senate races. And—well, it is a good question for all three of you. What role do you think the Federal Government could play in the 2018 elections?

Mr. PAINTER. So, the things I have laid out, and I am not the only one. Rick Ledgett and others have talked about this in the past. You know, a strong, clear declaratory statement that this is unacceptable and we will take action, a task force that is an interagency task force to work on this and also to deal with other parties, and particularly social media and others, working as has been happened, but working with the State and local election officials to actually secure their systems. I know DHS is doing some of that, but really up our game substantially there. Having the willingness to use tools to deter this action and actually having more tools there. That is just part of the response.

And then, frankly, working with other countries. Other countries are facing the same problem, not in 2018 elections, but in elections that they have. And maybe looking at some of the things they have done to push back against this and try to go after these disinformation campaigns.

The one thing I would say is this is not just a cyber problem, right? This has to be a hybrid solution to a hybrid threat. We have to have other players in the room, and not just the cyber people.

Mr. McCAUL. Well, I was in France right before Macron's election. I don't think the French bought into the propaganda. I was in Estonia and Ukraine. I mean, talk about a laboratory for malicious behavior. And I think we are learning a lot from that experience.

Mr. PAINTER. And I should mention that, as we stated earlier, Michael Sulmeyer has been working—Belfer has been working on some of these issues too, so I don't know if you address this quickly. I have taken all the time.

Mr. McCAUL. My time has expired, but I guess I am in the chair, so——

Mr. SULMEYER. Thank you for the opportunity to plug the Belfer Center, Chris. But that is why we have devoted work over the last year to try and help State and local officials and also campaigns just protect themselves and be harder to hack in the absence of

Federal Government doing a lot over the last year. So I would like to see, in terms of collection priorities, threats to the election be at the top. I don't know where they are. I am not in. But then I would like to make sure that there is a willingness to neuter attackers before they strike abroad. Then I would like to be able to see the willingness to reducing classification or declassify information that should get into the hands of those who can use it, make it action-able, and defend themselves.

Mr. MCCAUL. That is very good.

Let me just say in closing that, first of all, Chris, you did a fan-tastic job at State as the coordinator for cyber since—I guess 2011 is when that was created. Secretary Tillerson then tried to merge that office with the Bureau of Economic and Business Affairs. And I—they are sort of an interim step. But in my judgment, as I try to create a cyber agency within DHS, it almost appeared as if it was not a priority if you are merging it with another office like that. I would like to see a cyber office that makes it a priority. And I think that is what the Cyber Diplomacy Act that I worked with the chairman on to codify the Office of Cyber issues led by a Sen-ate-confirmed Ambassador precisely what we are trying to do here, is elevate the priority and the mission within the State Depart-ment.

Do all three of you agree with this bill?

Mr. PAINTER. I completely agree with this. I think the bill's for-mulation is absolutely correct. I know the State Department just today sent a letter saying they were going to create a Bureau deal-ing with some of these issues, which is great. However, the way its reporting structure is through the economic Under Secretary which, given the breadth of these issues and the security issues, doesn't make a lot of sense. I think the bill's statement should be through the political Under Secretary or higher makes a lot more sense as a cross-cutting issue. But I think that bill, frankly, helped motivate some of these changes, and that is good. We need to really keep the pressure on.

Mr. MCCAUL. That is good.

Mr. Miller.

Mr. MILLER. Thank you, Chairman McCaul, for now anyway, right?

Yeah, I also—and we, ITI, agree with the stated objectives of the Cyber Diplomacy Act. And those probably don't need any repeating here. But also the proposed follow-through on actually how you are going to keep the Internet open and free, while also protecting se-curity and promoting data flows.

One of the things that is really important about that is, number one, having a State Department cyber coordinator's office that real-ly is focused on the cyber issues. And we have heard that here today. But then also, the bill suggests the necessary follow-through. As Mr. Painter mentioned earlier, there was a lot of good progress made, both bilaterally and multilaterally in recent years by State. But you need to hold the counterparties accountable for the agree-ments that they are signing. And we really need to keep furthering these types of approaches, because these issues are not getting easier, they are getting harder and we need to be working together on this with our allies.

Mr. McCAUL. I agree completely.

Dr. Sulmeyer.

Mr. SULMEYER. Same answer but different reason, if I might offer, which is that from an interagency or non-State Department perspective, having a dedicated office like Chris Painter ran, gives you the touch point. You know who to call when you are at DOD or you are at a different part of the government. And that is how policymaking works is not always at the Secretary level but also at the lower levels of the bureaucracy. So I am a big supporter of this for additional reasons, because it helps the rest of the government come together and play as a team.

Mr. McCAUL. Yeah. I mean, it is just a point of contact, I think, for other departments.

Well, anyway, I want to thank all of you for your testimony and your expertise and leadership on this very important issue. I think it is very often overlooked as some sort of technical in-the-ether type thing. But in reality it is very real, and it is a threat on many levels, so I appreciate your leadership on this issue.

And with that, the committee now stands adjourned.

[Whereupon, at 12:58 p.m., the committee was adjourned.]

APPENDIX

MATERIAL SUBMITTED FOR THE RECORD

FULL COMMITTEE HEARING NOTICE
COMMITTEE ON FOREIGN AFFAIRS
U.S. HOUSE OF REPRESENTATIVES
WASHINGTON, DC 20515-6128

Edward R. Royce (R-CA), Chairman

February 6, 2018

TO: MEMBERS OF THE COMMITTEE ON FOREIGN AFFAIRS

You are respectfully requested to attend an OPEN hearing of the Committee on Foreign Affairs to be held in Room 2172 of the Rayburn House Office Building (and available live on the Committee website at http://www.ForeignAffairs.house.gov):

DATE: Tuesday, February 6, 2018

TIME: 10:00 a.m.

SUBJECT: U.S. Cyber Diplomacy in an Era of Growing Threats

WITNESSES: Mr. Christopher Painter
Commissioner
Global Commission for the Stability of Cyberspace
(*Former Coordinator for Cyber Issues, U.S. Department of State*)

Mr. John Miller
Vice President for Global Policy and Law, Cybersecurity, and Privacy
Information Technology Industry Council

Michael Sulmeyer, Ph.D.
Director
Cyber Security Project
Belfer Center for Science and International Affairs
John F. Kennedy School of Government
Harvard University
(*Former Director for Plans and Operations for Cyber Policy, Office of the Secretary of Defense, U.S. Department of Defense*)

By Direction of the Chairman

The Committee on Foreign Affairs seeks to make its facilities accessible to persons with disabilities. If you are in need of special accommodations, please call 202/225-5021 at least four business days in advance of the event, whenever practicable. Questions with regard to special accommodations in general (including availability of Committee materials in alternative formats and assistive listening devices) may be directed to the Committee.

COMMITTEE ON FOREIGN AFFAIRS
MINUTES OF FULL COMMITTEE HEARING

Day **Tuesday** Date **02/06/2018** Room **2172**

Starting Time **10:09AM** Ending Time **12:57PM**

Recesses **1** (*11:09AM* to *11:52AM*) (____ to ____) (____ to ____) (____ to ____) (____ to ____) (____ to ____)

Presiding Member(s)

Chairman Edward R. Royce
Representative Michael McCaul

Check all of the following that apply:

Open Session ☑
Executive (closed) Session ☐
Televised ☑

Electronically Recorded (taped) ☑
Stenographic Record ☑

TITLE OF HEARING:

U.S. Cyber Diplomacy in an Era of Growing Threats

COMMITTEE MEMBERS PRESENT:

See attached.

NON-COMMITTEE MEMBERS PRESENT:

N/A

HEARING WITNESSES: Same as meeting notice attached? Yes ☑ No ☐
(If "no", please list below and include title, agency, department, or organization.)

STATEMENTS FOR THE RECORD: *(List any statements submitted for the record.)*

IFR - Chairman Edward Royce
SFR - Representative Gerry Connolly
QFR - Representative Ted Lieu

TIME SCHEDULED TO RECONVENE __________
or
TIME ADJOURNED **12:57PM**

Full Committee Hearing Coordinator

HOUSE COMMITTEE ON FOREIGN AFFAIRS
FULL COMMITTEE HEARING

PRESENT	MEMBER
X	Edward R. Royce, CA
X	Christopher H. Smith, NJ
X	Ileana Ros-Lehtinen, FL
X	Dana Rohrabacher, CA
X	Steve Chabot, OH
X	Joe Wilson, SC
X	Michael T. McCaul, TX
	Ted Poe, TX
	Darrell Issa, CA
	Tom Marino, PA
	Mo Brooks, AL
	Paul Cook, CA
X	Scott Perry, PA
X	Ron DeSantis, FL
	Mark Meadows, NC
X	Ted Yoho, FL
	Adam Kinzinger, IL
X	Lee Zeldin, NY
	Dan Donovan, NY
	James F. Sensenbrenner, Jr., WI
X	Ann Wagner, MO
X	Brian J. Mast, FL
X	Brian K. Fitzpatrick, PA
	Francis Rooney, FL
X	Thomas A. Garrett, Jr., VA
	John Curtis, UT

PRESENT	MEMBER
X	Eliot L. Engel, NY
X	Brad Sherman, CA
	Gregory W. Meeks, NY
X	Albio Sires, NJ
	Gerald E. Connolly, VA
X	Theodore E. Deutch, FL
X	Karen Bass, CA
X	William Keating, MA
X	David Cicilline, RI
X	Ami Bera, CA
X	Lois Frankel, FL
	Tulsi Gabbard, HI
X	Joaquin Castro, TX
X	Robin Kelly, IL
	Brendan Boyle, PA
	Dina Titus, NV
X	Norma Torres, CA
X	Brad Schneider, IL
	Tom Suozzi, NY
X	Adriano Espaillat, NY
X	Ted Lieu, CA

THE SECRETARY OF STATE

WASHINGTON

FEB 6 - 2018

The Honorable
Edward R. Royce, Chairman
Committee on Foreign Affairs
House of Representatives
Washington, DC 20515

Dear Mr. Chairman:

Cyberspace policy affects almost every aspect of modern American life and it is a critical foreign policy imperative. With increasing incidents of disruptive global cyber attacks, including some sponsored by nation states, and the emergence of the digital economy dependent on internet connectivity, U.S. international leadership in this area will be important in the years to come. The Department of State must be organized to lead diplomatic efforts related to all aspects of cyberspace.

Over the last several months, we have engaged employees within relevant Department of State offices, invited the input of our partners across the federal interagency, and met with leading cyber experts and practitioners outside of the government to ensure that the Department's structure and policies would be well-informed and prepared for future technology challenges. The enclosed proposal will cohesively unify the Office of the Coordinator for Cyber Issues and the Bureau of Economic Affairs' Office of International Communications and Information Policy.

The combination of these offices in a new Bureau for Cyberspace and the Digital Economy will align existing resources under a single Department of State official to formulate and coordinate a strategic approach necessary to address current and emerging cyber security and digital economic challenges. The proposal will elevate the stature of the Department official leading cyberspace policy to one that is confirmed by the U.S. Senate – an Assistant Secretary – to lead high-level diplomatic engagements around the world.

The Assistant Secretary will report to the Under Secretary for Economic Growth, Energy, and the Environment. This placement in the Department's structure will ensure close coordination with the other bureaus that report to the Under Secretary and focus on functional policy issues while closely coordinating with the private sector. It will also give the Department the most effective platform from which to engage relevant global stakeholders.

The Department recognizes the keen interest of Members of Congress in cyberspace diplomacy and welcomes your input on, and support for, this proposal. As the Department proceeds with planning for this proposal, we will provide the requisite advance congressional notification of related reprogrammings consistent with applicable provisions of the State Department Basic

Authorities Act of 1956 and the annual Department of State, Foreign Operations, and Related Programs Appropriations Act. Please let my staff or me know if you would like to discuss this proposal.

Sincerely,

Rex W. Tillerson

Enclosure:
    As stated.

Cyberspace and Digital Economy Proposal

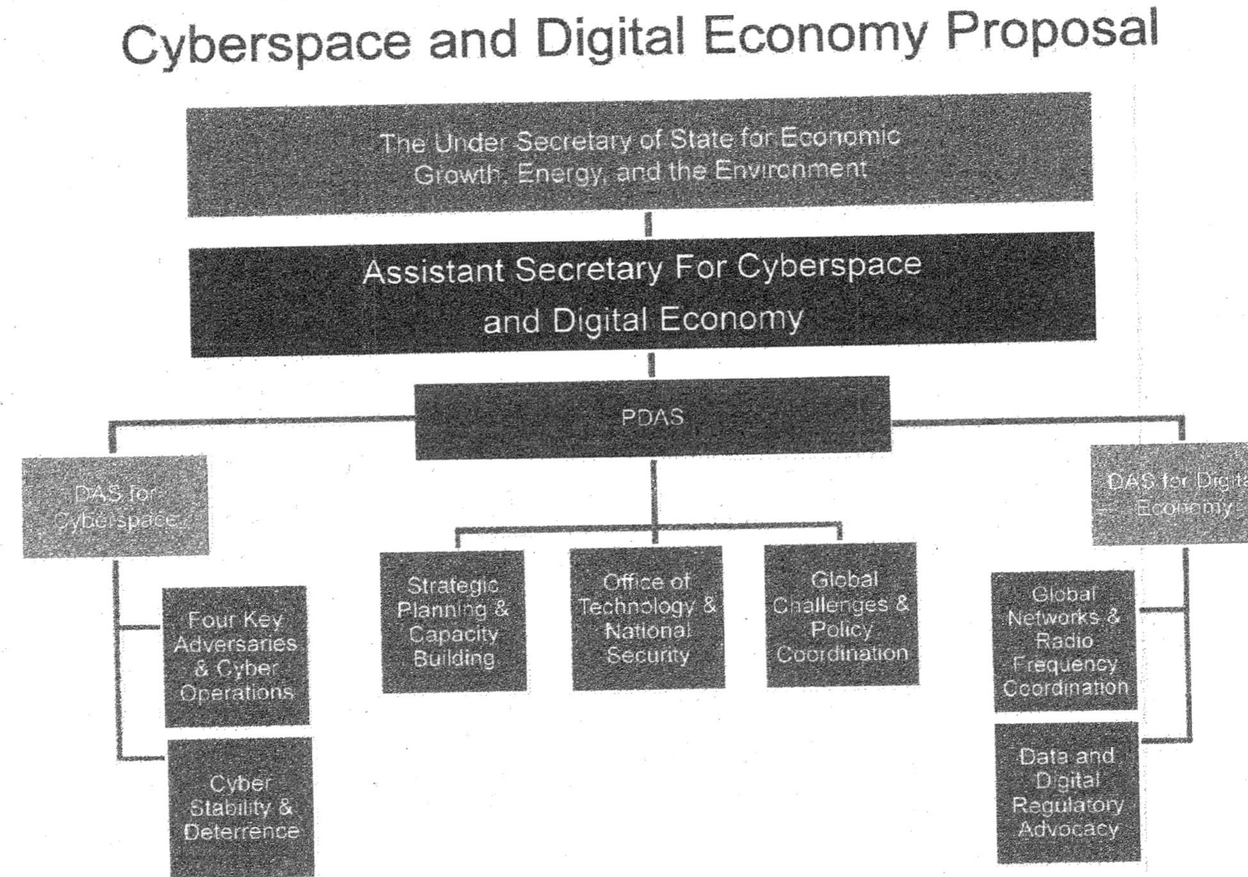

Primary Lines of Effort:

- **Establish a global deterrence framework** in which participating States make a political commitment to work together to impose consequences on States that engage in malicious cyber activities, based on participating States' shared understanding of what constitutes responsible State behavior in cyberspace.

- **Develop and execute key adversary specific strategies** to impose costs and alter calculus of decision-makers

- Advise and **coordinate external responses to national-security-level cyber incidents**

- Promote adoption of national processes and programs that **enable foreign territorial cyber, threat detection, prevention, and response**

- **Build foreign capacity to protect the global network** thereby enabling **like-minded** participation in deterrence framework

- **Maintain open and interoperable character of the Internet** with multi-stakeholder governance, instead of centralized government control

Primary Lines of Effort (continued):

- **Promote an international regulatory environment** for technology investments and the Internet that benefits U.S. economic and national security interests

- **Promote cross-border flow of data** and combat international initiatives which seek to impose restrictive localization or privacy requirements on U.S. businesses.

- **Protect the integrity of U.S. and international telecommunications infrastructure** from foreign-based threats. Serve as the USG interagency coordinator for international engagement. (Note: DHS and DoD lead on domestic-based threats.)

- **Secure radio frequency spectrum** for U.S. businesses and national security needs

- **Facilitate the exercise of human rights, including freedom of speech and religion**, through the Internet

- **Build capacity of U.S. diplomatic officials** to engage on these issues

Efficiencies:

- Strategic planning sets priorities for international engagements

- Cohesively unifies cyber security and digital economic policy development and implementation under a single chain of command

- Experts are shared, where possible, between cyber security and digital policy

- Cyber and digital economy efforts coordinated with regional bureau strategic plans

- CT continues primary lead on combatting terrorists' use of the Internet

- DRL has primary responsibility for implementing Internet freedom programming

- Coordination with INL on capacity building

- Deploy FSOs as expanded workforce for routine engagements

83

Statement for the Record
Submitted by Mr. Connolly of Virginia

The goal of U.S. cyber diplomacy operations must be to promote an open and secure internet that supports human rights, democracy, and the rule of law. Additionally, U.S. leadership of multilateral action on communication and information technology innovation ensures that international efforts to confront the evolving nature of transnational cyber threats serve the national security interests of the United States and our allies. The United States should be increasing our investment in cyber diplomacy to prevent and deter cyber attacks. Instead, the Trump Administration has not only neglected that investment, but also communicated to the rest of the world its willingness to deny the existence of this threat, which compounds U.S. vulnerability to future cyber intrusions.

Russia's unprecedented interference in the 2016 U.S. presidential election should have been a wake-up call. Our response should have consisted of three immediate actions: 1) Bolster our election infrastructure; 2) Demonstrate that there is a cost to those who engage in these attacks and deter them in the future; and 3) Work with our allies to share intelligence and best practices to protect our critical infrastructure from cyber attacks.

At our own peril, the Trump Administration and House Republicans have failed on each of these fronts. President Trump continues to deny Russia's interference in our election. Attorney General Jeff Sessions did not follow through on his own pledge to review how the United States can protect its elections from future Russian interference, and he could not identify specific actions that the Justice Department has taken to stop such interference. The Department of Homeland Security has refused to provide Congress with documents relating to Russian government-backed efforts to monitor, penetrate, or otherwise hack at least 21 state election systems in the 2016 election.

Despite near unanimous Congressional support for the Countering America's Adversaries Through Sanctions Act (P.L. 115-44), President Trump has neglected to use the authorities to sanction anyone involved in these attacks on American democratic institutions. Congress has refused to pass specific sanctions for election interference, or provide additional resources to harden our election systems. House Republicans have developed and executed a concerted attack on Special Counsel Robert Mueller's investigation into the Trump campaign's possible collusion with Russia, undermining the integrity of the FBI and DOJ in the process. Last week's release of Chairman Nunes' memo is just the latest salvo in the broader strategy to distract from and undermine the Russia investigation. The hardworking and patriotic employees of our law enforcement and intelligence agencies deserve better.

The Trump Administration has decimated the human resources, from the civilian workforce to senior leadership, that are critical to successful implementation of U.S. cyber diplomacy efforts. In July, Secretary of State Rex Tillerson closed the Office of the Coordinator for Cyber Issues. Tillerson missed the Trump Administration's own September deadline to develop an international strategy for cybersecurity cooperation. And Trump proposed an FY 2018 budget that would have gutted the State

Department's ranks and programs by one-third. These are not the actions of an Administration that takes seriously the threat of cyber attacks and the necessity of cyber diplomacy.

Last year, I reintroduced two bills that would address these threats. The FAST Voting Act (H.R. 1398) would strengthen the integrity of our voting system by incentivizing states to implement policy changes aimed at increasing voting system security. Ranking Member Engel and I introduced the SECURE Our Democracy Act (H.R. 530), which would publicly identify and authorize sanctions against foreign persons and governments that unlawfully interfere in U.S. federal elections.

Fortunately, there is at least some appetite in Congress to strengthen our federal cybersecurity infrastructure and lay the foundation for a robust cyber diplomacy campaign on a bipartisan basis. I have worked with my Republican colleagues to pass the Federal Information Technology Acquisition and Reform Act (FITARA) and the Modernizing Government Technology (MGT) Act to provide agencies with the foundation to make better IT acquisition investments and the money to upgrade their IT infrastructure. These investments are critical to bring our cybersecurity infrastructure into the twenty-first century. The House of Representatives recently passed Chairman Royce and Ranking Member Engel's Cyber Diplomacy Act of 2017, which I was glad to cosponsor. This legislation would establish a high-level Ambassador for Cyberspace to lead State's cyber diplomacy efforts and create a U.S. international cyber policy.

Russian interference in our 2016 elections was a powerful example of why we must work with our allies to gird our cybersecurity infrastructure, but it is not the only one. In an era of growing threats to cybersecurity, the United States must act now to make the necessary investments, develop a strategy, and conduct a robust campaign with our allies to protect U.S. national security. However, the rest of the world will not take us seriously as a leader on this front while the Trump Administration and House Republicans carry out a concerted effort to distract from and undermine our country's own investigation into the most high-profile cyber-enabled malicious activity ever directed at the United States by a foreign power.

Questions for the Record from Rep. Ted Lieu
U.S. Cyber Diplomacy in an Era of Growing Threats
February 6, 2018

Vulnerability Disclosure and Bug Bounty Programs:

Question:

Two years ago, the Department of Defense did what no other federal agency had ever done: It created a Vulnerability Disclosure Program that would allow security researchers to report cyber vulnerabilities they found on the .mil domains directly to DoD to fix them. It then also tacked on a high-profile Bug Bounty program called Hack the Pentagon to pay registered hackers to find vulnerabilities. Since then, the Department has received thousands of vulnerabilities, some of them very serious. **Based on your knowledge of the Hack the Pentagon program and industry best practices for improving an organization's cyber security, do you think the Department of State should follow suit and establish its own Vulnerability Disclosure Program and Bug Bounty Program?**

Answer:

Mr. Chris Painter's Response

I agree that the Vulnerabilities Disclosure Program and the DoD Bug Bounty program have been both innovative and effective. The officials at the State Department who deal with the technical protection of State Department systems are in the CIO's Office and in Diplomatic Security and so I would defer to them as to whether such a program could be effectively implemented by them. I would note however that effective implementation of such a program requires both personnel and financial resources (particularly for a "bounty" program, though a good argument could be made that initial expenditures are more than compensated for by longer term savings). I would also expect that there would be benefits to a more concerted government wide program with sharing of information between agencies, than each agency hosting their own. I assume that the current DOD program shares the vulnerability and other information they receive with DHS and other government agencies.

Mr. John Miller's Response

Bug Bounty programs have been useful in both the public and private sectors, employing "white hat" hackers to identify network vulnerabilities. In considering leveraging such hackers' expertise, it will be important to consult with the Department of Homeland Security (DHS) and consider the agency's role. DHS is responsible for protecting ".gov" networks. Specifically, the EINSTEIN system detects and blocks cyber attacks and provides DHS with insight into threats and vulnerabilities that may affect government networks more broadly and/or the private sector. I would recommend consulting with DHS cybersecurity experts to ensure that a Bug Bounty program would not conflict with or impede pre-existing government cybersecurity mechanisms.

<u>Dr. Sulmeyer's Response</u>

Government agencies would be wise to look to DoD's vulnerability disclosure program and its bug bounty program as models for improving cybersecurity. A fresh pair of eyes can discover flaws that even the most talented internal defenders may miss. However, before agencies implement programs like these, they must ensure that they are sufficiently resourced to address vulnerabilities that are reported. Otherwise, the risk that hackers will exploit these vulnerabilities increases over time.

As a next step, I would encourage the Department of State to assess the capabilities of its information technology workforce to remediate flaws within an appropriate time-frame after information about a vulnerability is submitted. Most vulnerabilities should be addressed within weeks of notification. If capabilities are lacking, the Department of State should provide an estimate of the resources necessary to expedite vulnerability mitigation. With an understanding of the Department of State's ability to address reported vulnerabilities, it should establish its own vulnerability disclosure and bug bounty programs.

Vulnerabilities Equities Process:

Question:

Last November, the Trump Administration released detailed information about the U.S.'s vulnerabilities equities process. This came after I introduced bipartisan, bicameral legislation called the PATCH Act to add transparency and oversight for the government process to decide when to disclose cyber vulnerabilities to the private sector to fix them. **Mr. Painter, can you describe the State Department's role in the vulnerabilities equities process and who represents the Department on the Equities Review Board (ERB)? In your view, is the new process sufficient for considering State Department equities?**

Answer:

<u>Mr. Chris Painter's Response</u>

I am pleased to see that the Administration has built on the Vulnerabilities Equities Process begun during the Obama Administration and has issued a detailed charter on this issue intended to increase organizational structure and transparency. Section 4.1 of that policy charter designates the State Department as one of the standing members of the "Equities Review Board" and states that each agency shall designate a POC who will in turn ensure that appropriate agency subject matter experts support discussions and determinations. As I left the Department prior to the release of this charter I do not know who the current State designee is to the board. However, since VEP decisions involve, among other things, technical, intelligence and policy factors, the POC and supporting experts should be able to weigh in on the full range of these issues. It appears that the charter does allow for full input by State and other agencies and, if there is a conflict, appeal through the normal NSC process.

Separately, I think it is important for other counties to also consider establishing and declare their own VEP processes given that this is not an issue that is unique to the U.S. Although the structural details of those processes may differ, having such a process, with as much procedural transparency as possible, is important to the protection of the global cyber ecosystem and to building trust and resilience, while, as appropriate, protecting national security and law enforcement equities.

<u>Mr. John Miller's Response</u>

To my knowledge, the vulnerabilities equities process maintains largely the same structure and process as during the previous administration. It includes representatives from all relevant agencies, particularly those with deep expertise in cyber and intelligence matters. My impression is that the State Department remains fully included in these meetings to address its equities and perspectives.